Japan

# Japan

**Jeff Kingston**

Polity

First published in 2019 by Polity Press

Polity Press
65 Bridge Street
Cambridge CB2 1UR, UK

Polity Press
101 Station Landing
Suite 300
Medford, MA 02155, USA

ISBN-13: 978-1-5095-2544-7
ISBN-13: 978-1-5095-2545-4(pb)

A catalogue record for this book is available from the British Library.

Library of Congress Cataloging-in-Publication Data

Names: Kingston, Jeff, 1957- author.
Title: Japan / Jeff Kingston.
Description: Cambridge ; Medford, Mass. : Polity Press, 2018. | Includes
    bibliographical references and index.
Identifiers: LCCN 2018011379 (print) | LCCN 2018022995 (ebook) | ISBN
    9781509525485 (Epub) | ISBN 9781509525447 (hardback) | ISBN 9781509525454
    (paperback)
Subjects: LCSH: Japan--Politics and government--1989- | Japan--Social
    conditions--1989- | Japan--Economic conditions--1989- | Japan--Foreign
    relations.
Classification: LCC DS891 (ebook) | LCC DS891 .K5385 2018 (print) | DDC
    952.05--dc23
LC record available at https://lccn.loc.gov/2018011379

Typeset in 11 on 13 Berkeley by Servis Filmsetting Ltd, Stockport, Cheshire
Printed and bound in Great Britain by Clays Ltd, Elcograf S.p.A.

For further information on Polity, visit our website: politybooks.com

"Let us be grateful to people who make us happy; they are the charming gardeners who make our souls blossom." – Marcel Proust

To Machiko, Goro and Zoe … heartfelt thanks to my wonderful and patient gardeners.

**The Japanese Archipelago**

# Contents

# 1

# Bouncing Back?

Japan enjoys an enviable reputation in the world, and most nations would love to have its problems, or at least what they know about them. A visiting MP from the United Kingdom, dazzled by the bustling prosperity and bright lights of twenty-first-century Tokyo, famously proclaimed, "If this is a recession, I want one." There is no gainsaying that Japan is a remarkable success story and has suffered far less social upheaval and glaring disparities than other advanced industrialized nations. In the global imagination, Japan is incredibly cool, mostly because of its pop culture of games, anime, manga, fashion, and cos play, in addition to *washoku* (Japanese food), cutting-edge technologies, vibrant traditions, and "lost in translation" off-beat wackiness. There is little violent crime, people are usually considerate and polite, streets are clean, and things seem well organized. In what other country would a rail company apologize for a train departing 20 seconds early?

This positive montage of images is accurate as far as it goes but is somewhat misleading and tidies away lots of other aspects of a society going through some major upheavals. Had the British MP travelled to Japan's provincial towns, his bubbly optimism would have confronted the depressing sight of *shattagai*, downtown shopping arcades where the shutters are permanently down on storefronts because of bleak economic conditions. There is a sense of crisis among many Japanese about their own futures and that of their nation. According to polls, Japanese are pessimistic and not especially happy compared to other nations. There are many reasons why, and one may be that how Japanese respond to a question may differ from how people in other nations respond. People are conditioned by their cultures and in some societies it may be more natural or acceptable to admit happiness or feel obliged to seem content. Japanese society is a pressure cooker, where people are driven by norms, expectations, and rules of conduct that are inculcated from a young age and reinforced in schools, the local community, and the workplace. Much is implicit, requiring people to read the situation and left wondering if they have done so correctly. None of this is unique to Japan, but with the exception of South Korea, I know of no other society that is quite so relentlessly intense or actively reinforces self-doubt to such a degree. It's not that people are not joyful or lacking in exuberance, but lots of this fades over the years as parents, teachers, neighbors, friends, colleagues, and bosses give meaning to the common expression: the nail that sticks out gets hammered. The hammering can be incessant and often self-administered as people work to fit in and not attract attention. This helps explain why there is often severe culture shock for returnees, those who have come back to Japan after living overseas. There are even special programs to ease the strains of re-entry for them.

The education system requires intensive swatting that places a premium on rote memorization to pass exams that very early on play a very influential role in deciding one's future. The fierce competition to get into the best junior high schools, high schools, and universities takes a toll on youth, justified by the common belief that such mind-numbing memorization and dedication will pay off in terms of the most desirable job offers. Self-sacrifice for the common good is a much-lauded virtue, one that helps employers pressure workers into working overtime for free (*sabisuzangyo*) and working excessive hours at the expense of their private life and health, sometimes to the point of death from overwork (*karoshi*). Over the past 30 years of living here, I sense these pressures are receding somewhat and there is more tolerance for diversity, respect for private lives and individual aspirations, but it is easy to come up with counterexamples. Strictly enforcing hair color rules in schools? Really? One Osaka high school student sued the prefectural government in 2017 because her school demanded that she dye her naturally brown hair black if she wanted to attend classes. Others have been excluded from yearbooks if they colored their hair. Advocates of such strict regulations that can cover skirt length, perming hair, and makeup argue that these rules help students avoid "getting lost" and prepare them for work and the need to abide by social norms.

Perhaps, in addition to such specific causes of unhappiness, there is a collective inclination to melancholy arising from *mono no aware* – an appreciation of the transitory nature of our world. This aesthetic is celebrated every spring with cherry blossom-viewing parties featuring various degrees of boisterous inebriation, poetic musings, and an ineffable foreboding because everyone knows that soon the blossoms will scatter in the wind. This is not to buy into the argument that Japan has a unique national character or that culture is destiny, but rather to suggest that such factors are relevant to better comprehend how Japanese see themselves and how some of them seek to explain Japan to others.

In my experience, people here are not generally prone to a "let the good times roll" mentality because this is a society that has experienced more than its share of devastating adversity – natural and manmade disasters – so when things are going well it's time to imagine it won't last. It is a land rich in expressions that convey resilience precisely because there has long been a need to have such a spirit. In the weeks after the March 11, 2011 monster tsunami that pulverized villages along the northeast coast of Tohoku, a relatively poor region known for a hardscrabble life, I often heard the expressions *gaman zuyoi* (stoic perseverance) and *nana korobi yaoki* (knocked down seven times get up eight times).[1] Such expressions were invoked so much that it began to annoy my relatives in the region who complained that it was just a way for the government to justify reducing relief and recovery assistance and leave them to their own devices. Possibly so, but I suspect that there is also local pride in what these expressions evoke: "we are tough and will bounce back."

There is a temptation for non-Japanese to invoke concepts that make sense to them to make sense of what is going on in Japan. For example, there is a rich literature that analyzes Japan in terms of modernization, using Western examples as benchmarks to evaluate what they observe. Certainly, Japan has been influenced and inspired by Western practices and institutions, especially since the intensification of globalization that has ensued from the heyday of imperialism in the late nineteenth century. And some Japanese also have tried to make sense of their nation's tremendous socioeconomic transformation from Tokugawa era (1602–1858) feudalism, in terms of Marxist and modernization theories. Useful no doubt, but in this short book, I aim to zoom in on the key forces, developments, and events that have characterized Japan's post-WWII trajectory. Rather than getting too caught up with modernization, the inevitable tensions with tradition and the predictable paradoxes to which this gives rise, we will focus on some of the major themes and contested issues of the past 70 years to show how they have shaped Japan and its place in the world today.

The ongoing transformation of Japan is the third in the modern era following the Meiji Restoration in 1868 and the US Occupation of 1945–52. Those reinventions of Japan were top-down and were both swift and sweeping, accomplished by decree, and unimpeded by significant opposition.[2] The US imposed liberal norms, democratic values, and civil rights that limited state power, while trying to empower women.[3] This prompted Prime Minister Yoshida Shigeru[4] to quip, "*Demokurushi*" (making a wordplay on the Japanese pronunciation of democracy) meaning, "But it is painful." As we will see, the contemporary overhaul is fitful, incremental, and contested in a nation where egalitarian, pacifist, and democratic values have become deeply entrenched following defeat in the Pacific War (1931–45). The most sweeping changes are evident in current Prime Minister Abe Shinzo's national security policy. The Abe Doctrine involves easing and bypassing constitutional constraints on Japan's armed forces and overturning the nation's embrace of postwar pacifism despite widespread public opposition. Article 9 of the constitution that renounces war and maintaining armed forces has become a talismanic touchstone of national identity. But to some conservatives, it is a humiliating reminder of defeat and subordination. What was inconceivable 20 years ago has happened rather quickly since 2013, although those on the hawkish end of the spectrum feel it is overdue, urgently essential, and just the beginning.

At the dawn of 2018, the Japanese media was abuzz

about Abe's plans to: (1) revise the pacifist constitution; (2) retrofit two large flattop vessels currently used for helicopters into aircraft carriers for deployment of stealth fighters; (3) expand purchases of stealth fighters, cruise missiles, and antiballistic missile systems; and (4) enhance contingency planning for conflict in the Korean peninsula in the National Security Council, a body that didn't even exist before 2013. The aircraft carriers, and cruise missile armed aircraft, would give Japan offensive military capabilities that the nation has sworn off for the past seven decades due to constitutional curbs.

This momentous shift on security under Abe is driven by China's regional hegemonic ambitions and North Korea's nuclear weapons program. Advocates argue that enhancing the nation's military capabilities is prudent given the evolving threat environment, while critics charge that this pivotal U-turn is unconstitutional, recklessly sacrificing non-militarist values that have served Japan well since WWII and transforming Japan into a full-blown military ally of the US with all the dangers that entails. Advocates counter that the US–Japan alliance has been lopsided, with the US committing to the defense of Japan without any reciprocal obligation. In light of President Donald Trump's "America First" policy, the Abe camp asserts that Japan risks weakening the alliance if it doesn't reciprocate, precisely at a time when the US security umbrella has become even more essential.

Battles over the US alliance and Japan's security

policy have persisted since the late 1950s. This political fault line extends to ongoing battles over wartime history, with liberals condemning the devastation inflicted on Asia and Japan, and supporting a forthright reckoning that conservatives oppose. Japan's rampage in Asia looms large over contemporary debates about the wisdom of abandoning the pacifist principles favored by liberals. Revisionists like Abe counter that this focus on Japanese depredations is masochistic, and they seek to restore pride in the nation by rehabilitating the wartime past. These cultural wars about national identity regarding history, security, and constitutional revision have intensified under Abe, whose economic policies are far less contentious.

The Japanese economy has been in the doldrums since the early 1990s, due to a combination of the asset bubble implosion, inconsistent macroeconomic policymaking, an aging society, and low productivity in the service sector. Social and economic problems festered, deepening the economic hole Japan needs to climb out of. Zigzagging on fiscal stimulus and austerity sharpened and prolonged the downturn, a legacy that is targeted by the bold policies of Abenomics – massive monetary easing, fiscal stimulus, and structural reforms. The jury is still out on Abenomics despite a soaring stock index and low unemployment because it is not clear whether it is overcoming deflation, improving household welfare, boosting productivity, or propelling sustainable growth. This is urgent business as Japan's demographic challenge of an aging and shrinking population confronts the government, firms, and households with grim prospects. Reviving Japan's economic dynamism is thus essential to address these interrelated problems.

Japan's enormous challenges – economic, demographic, security, and globalization – are driving the "third transformation," a work in progress involving a series of reforms that considered on their own seem of little consequence, but taken together represent an ambitious undertaking to reinvent Japan.[5] Since the early 1990s Japan has been in a prolonged period of transition in which subtle changes co-exist with prominent continuities. Reform has not been a linear process, onward and upward, relying more on pragmatic compromises and fine-tuning than shock therapy and sweeping measures. Yet, Japan in 2018 is very different from the way it was in 1988 during the frothy bubble era; over these fleeting three decades of my residence in Tokyo, many of Japan's seemingly ineradicable verities, assumptions, and practices have been reconsidered, revamped and, in some cases, cast aside.

There is an ebbing confidence about future prospects and a degree of fatalism about the nation's galloping demographic decline. The greying of Japan, and its shrinking population, constitute the nation's biggest and most intractable set of challenges. The fact that adult diapers have been outselling baby diapers since 2012 vividly conveys the dynamics. As of 2018, 27 percent of the population is over 65 years of age, and this ratio will nearly double by 2050, posing serious fiscal challenges in terms of spiraling budgets for national pensions, medical insurance, and elderly care. Dire population projections suggest that by 2050 the overall population could possibly shrink to 100 million from 127 million in 2000. How will so many fewer workers support the pensions and health care of so many more retirees? The ramifications of a shrinking domestic market for Japanese businesses are also alarming.

The stark implications of this demographic time bomb are covered extensively in the media, heightening the malaise that has gripped Japan since the stock and land asset bubble popped in the early 1990s. The subsequent implosion in values wiped out trillions of yen and cut a swathe of destruction through corporate Japan, leaving millions of households saddled with negative equity, precipitating the "lost decades." While the economic pain is undeniable, there have been many positive "losses" as well. In the aftermath, the Japan, Inc. system of close and cooperative relations between business and government, and the presiding elite lost considerable credibility and the public began to lose faith. The flailing response to the massive economic problems discredited the ways and means of a system that no longer seemed to have the answers for Japan's emerging problems. People demanded more transparency and accountability in government affairs, and by 1999 every major municipality, and the national government, had passed information disclosure legislation that enabled the media and people to better monitor what the government was doing. As scandals emerged about embezzlement and misappropriation of funds, taxpayers were outraged that cosseted bureaucrats were enjoying the highlife on the public purse. It also became clear that politicians and officials were routinely complicit in the rigging of public works contracts (*dango*) by construction firms in exchange for lucrative rake-offs. The waxing loss of faith in government also propelled a flowering of civil society, especially after the 1995 Kobe earthquake due to the government's incompetent disaster response.[6]

Previous reverence for public officials evaporated on the strength of so many damning revelations. It dawned on people just how risky it is to leave things up to a governing elite enjoying a cocoon of power and privilege, shielded from scrutiny. What had been business as usual under Japan, Inc. no longer met public expectations, thus raising the bar for good governance. Certainly, shady practices persist in twenty-first-century Japan, but new norms are being established, contested and mainstreamed in ways that are part of the quiet transformation. Gradually, the governing elite is being nudged and dragged into heeding these new norms and expectations even as it tries to evade them. The role of civil society provides another barometer of change. Non-profit organizations (NPOs), non-government organizations (NGOs), and volunteerism were an afterthought in responding to the Kobe disaster, but now are fully integrated into disaster emergency response preparations, and played an essential role in the March 2011 tsunami relief and recovery efforts.[7]

But while much remains to be done, the magnitude of what has already been achieved provides the most accurate barometer of Japan's ongoing third transformation. Japanese people, organizations and policymakers are responding to various challenges in diverse ways, though vested interests continue to protect their turf and fend off reforms. Japan. Inc. remains resilient, finding inspiration in adversity while advocating neoliberal reforms to awaken the animal spirits of capitalism by paring back regulations and taxes on business, reducing civil liberties, welfare and workers' legal protections, and making people more self-reliant (*jiko sekinen*). This amplifies risk in a society that is risk averse and promotes greater reliance on families rather than the state in times of need. The Japanese are divided and ambivalent about the ongoing renovation and unsure how to proceed, disappointed in the Establishment, but without viable alternatives. In the chapters that follow I paint a necessarily brief account of Japan's improbable rollercoaster journey from the devastation of 1945 through to the ongoing third transformation under Prime Minister Abe Shinzo. In doing so, I hope to give readers a stronger sense of Japan's rich postwar history and an appreciation of the pluck of a people and nation looking to bounce back – *nana korobi yaoki* – and become a more influential force in global affairs. While the mainstream consensus forecasts a genteel decline, technological innovation and medical breakthroughs offer glimmers of hope. Moreover, Japan, Inc. is not constrained by national borders and in expanding its footprint abroad and growing overseas, it may reinvigorate the nation and prove the doomsayers wrong. After all, in the mid-nineteenth century and again in 1945, Japan overcame bleak prospects and exceeded even the wildest expectations, so it may be too soon to start humming the nation's requiem.

# 2

# Japan, Inc.

In many respects Japan is a stunning success story, recovering speedily from wartime destruction and wowing the world with an economic miracle of double-digit annual GDP growth from the late 1950s to the late 1960s. While other industrialized national economies stagnated in the 1970s and experienced the social pathologies associated with high unemployment and growing income inequalities, Japan seemingly leapt from one milestone to another. It was an onward and upward story that far exceeded what anyone could have imagined gazing across the rubble of Tokyo in 1945.

Japan now boasts the third largest economy in the world, some of the world's most recognizable brands, and cutting-edge high-tech firms that play an essential role in global supply chains. It is a prosperous nation that enjoys a high degree of social cohesion, equality, safety, and a good national health insurance system. Tokyo has the world's best public transport system, some stunning architecture (surrounded by a miasma of functional buildings) and is a mecca for food, fashion, and art. Japan's cool vibe blends natural beauty, resilient traditions, high-tech, and pop culture, but how did it get here?

## Planned Economy

Policies adopted by the US Occupation played a key role in jumpstarting Japan's economic resurgence. American policymakers resuscitated the 1940 dirigiste system that helped wartime Japan squeeze the maximum output out of limited resources.[1] This system gave wartime bureaucrats extraordinary discretionary power to guide and control a command economy ranging from allocation of resources to production and distribution, in a nation squeezed by sanctions and blockades. It helped sustain Japan's war effort against steep odds and subsequently proved indispensable to the US during the occupation years. After 1947, the Cold War shifted the American priorities from punitive policies to transforming Japan into a showcase of the superiority of capitalism over communism, and a military outpost to contain the Soviet Union.[2]

The 1940 system had its roots in the development model embraced by Japan in the late nineteenth century that telescoped its industrial revolution into a few decades. Rather than an Adam Smith free market, laissez-faire approach, Japan's Meiji oligarchs drew inspiration from the neo-mercantilist policies favored by Friedrich List, which relied on a strong state role in promoting development. Lagging far behind the Western imperial nations that had imposed unequal commercial treaties on Japan in the mid-nineteenth century, Meiji leaders understood the disadvantages of a free market approach. They promoted *fukoku kyohei* (rich nation, strong military) and knew that responding to the threat of Western imperialism required rapid economic growth to finance a sweeping military modernization.[3] Given shortages of capital and resources, and a sense of urgency, Japan adopted state-sponsored capitalism, where, in contrast to the Anglo-American model, the government took the lead in initiating and funding industrialization projects, and then privatized them. This helps explain some of the tensions and misunderstandings that ensued with growing bilateral trade tensions in the 1970s and 1980s; what looked like a rigged system to Washington, featuring cozy government–business ties, was a legacy of Meiji-era development policies and the 1940 system that the US had endorsed during the Occupation era.

To revive Japan, the US put in place a system that it came to regret. But given the abject state of the Japanese economy, tilting the playing field to the home team's advantage seemed a good idea because there was no support in the US for a Marshall Plan of aid to help Japan recover as there was in Europe in the aftermath of WWII. In the early years of the Occupation, Japan suffered from severe shortages of everything, and there was a rationing system for food that many families supplemented with visits to the thriving *yamiichi* (black markets). Gangs controlled the black markets, making hefty profits out of helping families get what they needed to survive. One judge, who starved to death by shunning the black market, was held up by some as an inspiring example of probity and by others as testimony to the folly of abiding by the rules.

In the aftermath of war, tax revenues did not cover mounting expenses, so the government began print-ing more paper money, sparking hyperinflation. Hyperinflation benefitted former tenant farmers by wiping out the value of their debts; the American land reform gave them the right to purchase the fields they had been sharecropping at a bargain price funded by long-term, low-interest loans. This land reform was perhaps the most beneficial policy enacted under the Occupation, transforming the desperate rural poor into a middle class suddenly given the wherewithal to become consumers. They helped boost demand for a range of consumer products manufactured in Japanese factories because now they could afford what had always been out of reach. This leveling of disparities in the countryside also promoted political stability and created a large and loyal constituency indebted to the ruling conservative politicians. In the decades since then, they have been reliable supporters of the Liberal Democratic Party (LDP) that has dom-inated postwar Japanese politics. This helps explain the longstanding government tolerance of dispari-ties in per capita Diet representation between thinly populated rural electoral districts and urban districts, which gives disproportionate weight to the votes of rural citizens who tend to favor the LDP. The Supreme Court ruled that this electoral system is unconstitu-tional due to the skewed representation, forcing some minor modifications since 2015 to reduce the malapportionment.

Millions of these new landowners were happy to see their debts suddenly erased by hyperinflation in the late 1940s, but the landowners who were forced to sell their land to them were left holding worthless money. More importantly, the evaporating value of currency was a nightmare for businesses because they could not properly plan in such an unpredictable environment. The Americans sent over banker Joseph Dodge who imposed a balanced budget that cut government spending drastically and reined in hyperinflation. Putting the brakes on so precipitously, however, sent the economy skidding into a ditch. It was only the outbreak of the Korean War in 1950, and large US military procurements, that rescued the economy from recession and launched it on a growth trajectory. Prime Minister Yoshida Shigeru (1946–7; 1948–54) reportedly called the war a "gift from the gods."

Aside from the land reform and Korean War, the US boosted Japanese growth by opening the US market to Japanese exporters. This was a critical factor in sustaining Japan's recovery and emergence as an industrial powerhouse. Moreover, resuscitating the 1940 system gave bureaucrats extensive powers to adopt protectionist measures that benefitted domestic producers by shielding them from competition. This system also bestowed informal discretionary powers of "administrative guidance" (*gyosei shido*) that enabled officials to advise firms about how they should operate. Firms could do otherwise, and some did, but there was an implicit understanding that defying the government might entail unpleasant consequences.

The Americans also helped by not proceeding with initial plans to dissolve the wartime *zaibatsu* (family-owned industrial conglomerates), an example of how Occupation policies involved a degree of compromise.[4] General Douglas MacArthur was the Supreme Commander of the Allied Powers (SCAP) and in this role had sweeping policymaking powers. He and his advisers were incensed that after Japan surrendered, the *zaibatsu* had raided state warehouses for scarce commodities that they then sold on the black market for lavish profits. It did not help that they were deemed complicit in Japan's war of imperial aggression and the US wanted to hold them accountable by breaking them up. But, unlike the landowners who had no clout in Washington to fend off land reform, the venerable *zaibatsu* had extensive ties with corporate America. Drawing on these connections, they lobbied Washington, asserting that if the anti-*zaibatsu* dissolution policies went forward, it would create economic chaos, benefit communists, and make Japan more dependent on sustained US financial support. Corporate America was more interested in reviving commercial ties than in reinventing Japan, so pressure was put on MacArthur to back off his cartel-busting plans. In the end, family control of *zaibatsu* was largely ended and they were reinvented as bank-centered industrial conglomerates (*keiretsu*) run by professional managers. So, famous *zaibatsu* such as Mitsui, Mitsubishi, Sumitomo, and Hitachi remained as influential corporate behemoths that continued to dominate the Japanese economy as they had done during the wartime era. By accommodating this continuity, the US left intact companies that had the expertise, networks, and wherewithal to make a rapid recovery possible under the guidance of empowered bureaucrats in Japan's managed market economy.

Industrial targeting was a key strategy of the developmental state.[5] This meant that the government would identify priority sectors and encourage private sector investments with public sector signaling through subsidized loans and developing related infrastructure. Knowing the government-backed projects in certain sectors, firms and banks understood that their related investments and loans would be safe and acted accordingly. In this way the government intervened extensively to shape the course of Japan's economic recovery. Given Japan's lack of natural resources, it did not make sense from a comparative advantage standpoint to prioritize heavy industry and petrochemicals, but because they had excellent potential, the government targeted them for development. The government was also keen to avoid excessive competition and allowed the operation of industrial cartels where producers had a free hand in setting prices and allocating market share.

By conferring extraordinary powers on the government and promoting close cooperation between the bureaucracy and business, the developmental state paradigm meant that Japan, Inc. was a hybrid command market economy where the government acted as arbiter and regulator while providing assistance in licensing foreign technology, allocating foreign exchange to pay for imports, distributing subsidies, promoting trade, and implementing various protectionist policies to limit foreign competition. Tariffs, quotas, and non-tariff barriers such as discriminatory regulatory requirements kept foreign competitors at bay while the government did not allow repatriation of profits, a huge disincentive for foreign firms since it meant they were required to invest any profits in Japan. Mistakes were made and the benefits of the developmental state have been overstated as industrial targeting worked better in certain sectors (steel, chemical, machinery, and electronics) than others; the auto industry is an example of a sector that defied guidance by the Ministry of International Trade and Industry (MITI) urging consolidation.[6] Picking winners was easier in sectors with established technologies, but far less so in cutting-edge or next-generation fields.[7] Overall, the cozy, cooperative, and sometimes collusive relations that defined Japan, Inc. proved effective,[8] facilitating a pragmatic approach that valued producers over consumers, but in some respects made a mockery of democratic governance, illustrated by an endless cascade of corruption scandals and influence peddling.[9]

Significantly, the role of the government in the economy evolved such that by the late 1970s it focused more on providing structural adjustment assistance to industries battered by rising oil prices and encouraging investment in R&D. Sharp increases in oil prices orchestrated by the Organization of Petroleum Exporting Countries (OPEC) propelled energy-intensive industries into crisis because they were totally dependent on imported oil and gas. Production processes and manufacturing operations that made sense with cheap oil, no longer looked viable. The government wanted to avoid mass layoffs and bankruptcies, thus opting for policies that muted market forces by subsidizing jobs and adopting other countermeasures targeting these "sunset industries" and permitting "recession cartels" that allowed competitors to fix prices and allocate market share. These countermeasures were implemented on a temporary basis to allow firms to adjust to the quadrupling of oil prices, but once adopted it never seemed there was a good time for politicians to end such schemes. While these policies were crucial to avoid massive economic dislocation and job losses, they also subsidized inefficiencies and represented a "misallocation" of resources in terms of market forces. But for the government, it was better to help Japan, Inc. preserve jobs than to cope with the problems of high unemployment that had devastated communities in Europe and the US. Keeping people in work and promoting the sense of security and loyalty associated with the lifetime employment system nurtured a high degree of social cohesion and preserved workers' dignity and skills. It is a complex calculus, but Japan lacked a social safety net for the jobless and the cost of providing welfare and job training would have been high. By outsourcing welfare to Japan, Inc. and helping firms keep faith with their workers during the inevitable business cycle fluctuations, the government kept workers on the job, paying taxes, and supporting their families.

But there is no free lunch. Preserving jobs in industries that were no longer competitive may have been beneficial in the short term, but it also meant subsidizing inefficiencies and sustaining investments in sectors that faced difficult prospects. In this way the developmental state helped Japan, Inc. postpone the reckoning, masking problems and disadvantaging firms that relied on relatively costly domestically produced components.[10] Firms within the same *keiretsu* would steer their business to other member firms while manufacturers relied on longstanding domestic production chains when purchasing inputs. Japan was a relatively closed economy, meaning that producers often relied extensively on less efficient, relatively high cost Japanese producers for inputs that could be imported from overseas producers at a lower price for similar quality. This cost disadvantage was a burden, especially on Japanese export-oriented producers that had to compete in global markets. Firms offset this disadvantage by selling goods domestically at higher prices than in global markets, a practice called dumping.

In order to secure market share in overseas markets, domestic consumers were gouged to help subsidize exports. Such practices are not allowed under current trade rules but were fairly common until the WTO banned them. Winning market share by rigging the system in this way shifted employment adjustments to trading partners. This stoked political tensions as rising trade imbalances in Japan's favor were seen as proof of unfair, predatory trading practices.

## Trade Frictions

From the late 1960s up through the 1990s, trade tensions between Japan and the US increased dramatically and became a source of mutual recriminations. President Nixon famously called on Prime Minister Sato Eisaku (1964–72) to lean on Japanese textile producers to rein in exports to the US because the flood of cheap, quality Japanese textiles was wreaking havoc in the textile belt in southeastern states that Nixon wanted to woo for Republican candidates and his own re-election. He offered a quid pro quo, return of Okinawa to Japanese control in exchange for limiting textile exports to the US and thought he had an understanding that Tokyo would cooperate when Sato's reply was mistranslated as "Yes." In fact, Sato had said "Hai, wakaremasita," or "Yes, I understand" which is often a polite way for Japanese to signal refusal. Nixon was furious when Japanese exports continued unabated, thinking that Sato had deceived him. On such a misunderstanding, bilateral relations suffered.

By the late 1970s, Japan's trade surplus with the US became a significant political issue. US Congressmen gathered in front of the Capitol and smashed Japanese products and made accusations that Japan engaged in unfair trade practices. In 1979 Harvard sociologist Ezra Vogel published *Japan as Number One*,[11] a book that became a bestseller in Japan where the kudos was welcome. It was salt in the wounds for an America that was taken by surprise by Japan's manufacturing prowess. Who could have imagined that American consumers would trade in their gas guzzling unreliable cars for Japan's reliable, fuel-efficient compact vehicles?

Chalmers Johnson's *MITI and the Japanese Miracle* explained how the developmental state had picked winners and helped them win. Rather than Adam Smith's invisible hand, he drew attention to the Japanese government's extensive and usually adroit intervention in helping Japan, Inc. He argued that it was time to end the Cold War bargain of the US encouraging Japanese economic success in exchange for Japan hosting US military bases. It was, in his view, an unfair deal that had outlasted its usefulness because the US was burdened with defending Japan and allowing unfettered access to the US market, policies that were unreciprocated. His "revisionist" analysis challenged the prevailing mainstream of generally admiring views about Japan expressed by most contemporary experts. Johnson's book was a sign of the times and his explanation of how the developmental state rigged the system resonated with American inclinations to blame the Japanese for "cheating" rather than acknowledge US shortcomings and Japanese advances.

While Washington criticized Japan for its mercantilist policies of orchestrating commercial success at the expense of the US, it also sought Tokyo's intervention to restrain exports and boost imports. This was not a market solution, but rather an attempt to get the developmental state to manage the bilateral trade relationship to lessen the adverse consequences for US producers and thereby mitigate political tensions. So, while criticizing Japan for managing trade, Washington also asked it to manage trade to benefit US producers, but such "voluntary export constraints" and "orderly marketing agreements" came at the expense of US consumers by boosting the prices of Japanese products such as automobiles to protect Detroit's inferior products.

In the 1985 Plaza Accord, after years of acrimonious accusations, Japan agreed to a sharp appreciation in the value of the yen as a means to reduce its massive trade surpluses. The idea was that a stronger yen would make Japanese products more expensive in importing countries and thereby reduce imports of Japanese goods and reduce trade deficits. In reality, Japanese exporters had nurtured brand loyalty by selling excellent products backed by superb service and those customers were not deterred by higher prices. Sony, for example, was beating US television producers like Zenith and Motorola because it made a vastly better product, and consumers appreciated the difference and were willing to pay a premium. So, the Plaza Accord failed to curb Japan's trade surpluses and they remained a significant problem in bilateral relations with the US. Those were the days when bookshops had shelves devoted to extolling the virtues of Japanese-style of management and the samurai work ethic, a preoccupation that now seems quaintly misinformed. At that time, Japan, Inc. still had great credibility, however, and following the 1987 collapse in world markets, Tokyo alone seemed relatively unscathed and agreed to act as an engine of global growth, lowering interest rates and pursuing stimulus polices to revive G7 economies. The developmental state juggernaut seemed unstoppable and the government appeared incapable of putting on the brakes. Karel van Wolferen drew attention to this flaw just as the Japanese economy swooned in the aftermath of the asset bubble collapse that Bill Emmott had predicted.[12] This crash in the early 1990s, when the overheated stock and real estate markets cratered, erased two-thirds of their 1989 peak value.

## Environmental Nightmare

The story of mercury poisoning suffered by residents near the port of Minamata in Kyushu is a well-known tale of corporate knavery and government complicity.[13] It is a grim example of the dark side of Japan's economic "miracle" and the price that people were made to pay in support of industrialization. The haunting pictures of the victims taken by Eugene Smith and published in *Life Magazine* and elsewhere in the early 1970s graphically depict the human consequences of growth at all costs. Minamata is not just a story of an environmental catastrophe, but is also a microcosm of postwar Japan and the evolving nature of citizenship and democracy in an increasingly prosperous nation.

Chisso's chemical factory continued to dump mercury into Minamata Bay even after it knew that anyone consuming local fish, including the infamous "dancing cats" who suffered neurological spasms, were being poisoned by the effluent. During Japan's post-WWII economic miracle, Chisso was a leading producer of acetaldehyde, expanding production seven-fold in the 1950s. A by-product was methyl-mercury, a highly toxic compound that was routinely dumped untreated into the adjacent bay until 1968. Mercury poisoning can lead to neurological disorders that weaken muscles, cause spasms, influence hearing and sight, and in extreme cases paralysis, coma, and mental illness. In pregnant women, mercury concentrated in the fetus, causing severe birth defects in their children.

Beginning in 1956, a local hospital reported to public health authorities that there was an epidemic among children suffering similar symptoms affecting the central nervous system. The government investigated the causes of the disease, calling on medical experts at Kumamoto University who found that the victims were clustered in fishing hamlets along the shoreline of Minamata Bay and in November 1956 concluded that they suffered from heavy metal poisoning caused by consumption of fish and shellfish. From the outset, Chisso was the main suspect as the source of contamination because its wastewater included many different heavy metals, but it was not until 1959 that researchers pinpointed methyl-mercury as the culprit. The concentrations of mercury were so high in the sludge of the bay near the factory's wastewater outlet that Chisso even established a subsidiary to recover and process it while at the same time denying responsibility for the local rash of neurological disorders that became known as Minamata Disease.

The cumulative pollution had destroyed the bay's ecosystem as seaweed no longer grew, fish stocks dropped by 90 percent, birds dropped from the skies and dead fish floated on the polluted water, all signs of an environmental catastrophe. The firm's in-house research confirmed that methyl-mercury was the cause, but management covered up this finding. The local government imposed a partial ban on the sale of fish from Minamata Bay, angering local fisherman because a partial ban meant Chisso was not required to pay them compensation. This became an ongoing theme – the interests of Chisso trumped those of its victims. The reason why is simple: Chisso was by far the largest taxpayer and employer in the town.

In 1959, the company built a waste-treatment facility that did nothing to reduce mercury levels, hoodwinking the parties involved and slowing efforts toward a real solution because everyone assumed that the problem had been resolved even as untreated effluent continue to pour into the bay. At a media event staged to open the facility, a top executive appeared to drink water that had been treated there, but in fact, the official drank uncontaminated water from another source because he knew that the "treated" wastewater was still unsafe. Subsequent government surveys conducted in 1960 and 1961 confirmed that mercury poisoning was widespread and ongoing, but these results were not made public.

It was not until 1968 that the government finally acknowledged the link between Chisso, methylmercury poisoning, and the outbreak of Minamata Disease. In 1973, the court decided in favor of the victims and awarded a record level of damages, but many victims who had not been recognized officially were left out of the settlement. The very strict criteria for official recognition, and pressures on certification committees to deny recognition as much as possible, were a major source of contention. The "unrecognized" victims struggled for something resembling justice into the twenty-first century. By 2004, Chisso paid some $86 million in total compensation to about 10,000 victims and was finally ordered to clean up the contaminated area. However, it was not until 2010 that an agreement was reached that covered a significant number of uncertified victims, bringing an end to this tawdry saga of corporate negligence.

Government officials in Tokyo were willing to look the other way because they did not want the suffering of small numbers of citizens in a remote village to endanger their grand plans for growth and industrialization. Local officials and some citizens didn't want to lose tax revenues and jobs, and worried that coming clean about the environmental disaster would condemn their town to decline and stigmatization. But this is also a story of how ordinary citizens fought for their rights and accountability and in the end, after half a century, with the help of the courts and media, won a degree of justice and vindication against the odds.

## The Bad Sleep Well

Kurosawa Akira's classic film *The Bad Sleep Well* (1961) depicts the nexus of corruption that is inherent to Japan's Iron Triangle (the LDP, big business, and the bureaucracy), and how high-ranking perpetrators are not held accountable for their malfeasance. The bad still sleep well, confident that they won't be prosecuted or jailed for their misdeeds because the

Establishment protects its own. The developmental state delivered rapid post-WWII economic recovery, but it has also been a hotbed of corruption. The cozy and collusive ties inherent to the Iron Triangle involve questionable practices and dubious ties, where moral hazard, regulatory capture, and corruption are rife. Influence peddling is common practice precisely because bureaucrats' extensive discretionary powers provide politicians ample scope to lobby for favors on behalf of vested interests and reap rewards for doing so.

Kurosawa's indictment of connivance between officials, construction company executives, and politicians still resonates in twenty-first-century Japan. In 2017, the media exposed bid rigging (*dango*) by the top four construction firms engaged in an $80 billion maglev train project. Back in 2005 when these same firms were caught in a similar scam to divide market share and boost contract prices, they pledged never to do so again, but the benefits of *dango* are hard to resist. Gouging clients to improve the bottom line is not unique to Japan but has been surprisingly resilient and apparently widespread. The agenda of greater transparency and accountability remains a work in progress, however, because it is a threat to the ways and means of Japan, Inc.

*Amakudari* (descent from heaven) is an institutionalized system of influence peddling by former bureaucrats who lobby their former colleagues on behalf of firms that hire them. Their "job," handsomely rewarded, is to help firms navigate the bureaucratic networks, gather information and convey requests. These officials face a conflict of interest when they are supervising organizations that they hope to get a job offer from after retiring. In order to curry favor, officials use their discretionary powers to confer favors they anticipate being subsequently reciprocated. This regulatory capture enables organizations to manipulate the system at the expense of the public interest. While these organizations may indeed try to game the system by hiring retiring insiders, they also feel pressure to do so, fearful of negative consequences if they don't.

Due to numerous scandals involving *amakudari*, there have been many attempts to ban it, but none have been successful. At its most benign, the practice is justified as a means of ensuring better communication between government and the private sector by creating networks of information sharing, but numerous scandals over the years and revelations about shady dealings and munificent compensation make it look more like a bureaucratic shakedown.

Why has this practice persisted for so long despite being banned and periodically censured? The largest loophole has been lax enforcement. Officials are charged with ensuring compliance within their own ministries and agencies, but it is hard to deny your colleagues what they consider their due since this is a longstanding practice. As prospects for further promotions dwindle, senior bureaucrats are eased out with an implicit promise of a post-retirement job. Thus, there are institutional imperatives that sustain a suspect practice and make it very difficult to curb because bureaucrats can be wily in sidestepping bans, aided and abetted by confederates who are supposed to crack down on the practice.

For example, in 2007 the Diet revised the National Public Service Law to prohibit serving bureaucrats from lobbying for post-retirement sinecures for their colleagues. This reform was enacted because there was a perception that *amakudari* was standard operating procedure and a hotbed for unethical practices. But the ban does not apply to retired officials lobbying for jobs on behalf of their former ministries and officials who have not yet retired. In 2017, an *amakudari* scandal engulfed the Ministry of Education when it emerged that the ministry sought to circumvent the legal ban by relying for several years on a retired bureaucrat to act as an ad hoc matchmaker between universities and the ministry's personnel department. Lists of retiring bureaucrats were provided and the ex-official facilitated their employment at universities. It was hard to refuse given how dependent universities are on the discretionary budgetary powers of ministry officials. Research funds, establishment of new departments, subsidies, caps on student enrollments, etc., are all subject to ministry approval, ensuring that universities understand the importance of allocating jobs to retiring officials. This system operated in a manner that indicates that those involved knew that they were circumventing the ban on *amakudari*, but figured they could do so with impunity.

*Amakudari* has been uncovered at several other ministries, most notably at the Ministry of Economy, Trade and Industry (METI) that oversaw the nuclear industry through its Nuclear and Industrial Safety Agency (NISA). Lax enforcement of regulations by NISA was a crucial factor in the Fukushima nuclear accident, and *amakudari* may have played a role as utilities and related companies were a hotbed of post-retirement jobs for retiring METI/NISA officials. Did regulators allow their desire for such a well-paid sinecure cloud their judgment? There are no smoking guns, but in the court of public opinion, regulators are in the dock alongside utility executives, viewed as culprits in what three major investigations conclude was a man-made tragedy owing much to slipshod safety practices and regulatory capture, whereby regulators regulated in favor of the regulated.

Influence peddling has sparked numerous other scandals in Japan from the early post-WWII era until the present. Perhaps the most notorious case was the Lockheed scandal that implicated Prime Minister Tanaka Kakuei (1972–74). He was paid to convince All Nippon Airways (ANA) to overturn its decision to purchase aircraft from McDonnell Douglas and instead order the planes from Lockheed. Marubeni, a top trading company, with help from Kodama Yoshio, a Class A war crimes suspect and rightwing fixer alleged to have mob ties, facilitated the influence peddling deal. The bribery details were revealed in Congressional hearings chaired by US Senator Frank Church in 1976 that were probing US companies making overseas payoffs to secure contracts. A senior Lockheed executive testified that a total of about $2 million was distributed to Japanese government officials through Marubeni. Tanaka was identified as the main culprit and arrested that summer on suspicion of violating the Foreign Exchange and Foreign Trade Act, sort of like Al Capone getting busted on tax evasion. He was Japan's first serving prime minister to be arrested for a criminal act. Illustrious predecessors like Yoshida Shigeru and Sato Eisaku had been implicated in domestic bribery scandals, but in those cases the Establishment circled the wagons, derailing efforts to prosecute them. Tanaka's humble background, lack of a university degree, or blueblood family connections made him expendable, especially since the cloud of money politics had dogged him since the outset of his career. He was a brash go-getter with a common touch who refined the dark arts of "fund raising," helping to finance the campaigns of many LDP colleagues and building the largest faction in his party. He represented the unscrupulous side of Japan, Inc., leveraging access to key bureaucrats into lucrative ties with companies that needed favors.[14] But in drawing international attention to a political system mired in corruption, Tanaka had crossed a line. Nonetheless, he was re-elected several times by his loyal Niigata constituency while his court case dragged on, but failing health finally lead to his ouster as faction head in the late 1980s. He remained a member of the Diet until 1990 and died in 1993. He was a giant in Japanese politics, nicknamed the Shadow Shogun, who stood out from the crowd of faceless leaders that dominated mainstream politics, and in 2016 mounted an unlikely posthumous comeback as the press and several books lauded his no-nonsense style while extenuating his venality.

## Recruiting Politicians

The Recruit scandal of the late 1980s brought down a government, tarnished the reputations of the powerful, and left the public convinced that government was rotten to the core. Recruit, a Tokyo-based human resources and employment company, distributed pre-flotation shares in a real estate subsidiary, Cosmos, to lawmakers and prominent figures in the business world in the mid-1980s. When Cosmos subsequently went public, its share-price rocketed, enriching those in on the scheme – allegedly including then Prime Minister Takeshita Noboru, former Prime Minister Nakasone Yasuhiro and future prime ministers Miyazawa Kiichi and Mori Yoshiro among several other politicians from across the political spectrum. In many cases, it was the politicians' private secretaries who received the shares, providing a barely plausible cover. Ezoe Hiromasa, the founder of Recruit, came to personify a squalid system of influence buying. His goal was to secure favorable regulatory changes for his business. He was an outsider to the cozy world of Japan, Inc.'s elite, so biddable politicians offered a way in.

The Asahi newspaper broke the story in June 1988. At the time nobody, least of all Ezoe, imagined that the original story about a deputy mayor of Kawasaki receiving shares in exchange for favors would snowball into such a massive scandal reverberating throughout the corridors of power, toppling the Takeshita cabinet and dominating the news through the end of the 1980s.

Ezoe's advisor suggested bribing a Diet member after the scandal broke as a way to stop him from asking awkward questions. The bribe offer was covertly videotaped and aired on TV, providing unambiguous evidence that Recruit was involved in a cover-up and guilty of trying to suborn a lawmaker. This was the smoking gun that convinced everyone that Ezoe was guilty.

Ezoe, who died in 2013, accused the media of sensationalism and prosecutors for wrongfully prosecuting him.[15] He was especially critical of how the media convicted him through innuendo, jumping to conclusions not merited by the evidence and failing to distinguish between legal and moral wrongdoing. He contended that his actions were legal and the case against him was based on moral outrage rather than the law. However, after a trial lasting 13 years, he was found guilty. Ezoe explained,

I was an example of the proverbial nail sticking up ready to be hammered. I think I appeared in various media too often – even in daytime tabloid TV shows. In addition, although I was brought up in a poor family, Recruit, the information company I founded, performed far better than other media companies including major newspaper companies and TV stations in terms of sales and profits. I think that is why I became a target of their attacks. In Japanese society, it is a tradition that those who were brought up in a family of pedigree are more respected than those who are not. (Interview August 2010)

Unrepentant, Ezoe decided to fight the prosecutors because he was angry at being coerced to sign inaccurate statements that unjustly implicated him and others. In seeking vindication, he defied social expectations, pointing out that, "Since old times in Japan there is an expectation that the accused will apologize and show remorse for his actions and then will be forgiven. But instead I chose to fight and thus I was never forgiven." Although he could have avoided judicial purgatory if he had plead guilty and apologized, Ezoe insisted it was worth fighting the charges because he was innocent and had to defend himself at all costs.

But was Ezoe innocent? Even though the distribution of stocks may not have been illegal and did not involve an explicit quid pro quo, in Japan one can hardly ignore expectations and obligations. The moral outrage targeting him was apparently triggered by jealous envy over his sudden wealth, his ostentatious lifestyle, and what appeared to be too clever exploitation of grey areas in the law. His actions offended social mores, as he manipulated the system and blatantly doled out favors, anticipating that powerful recipients would find themselves in a position to reciprocate in some way.

Ezoe manifests the seamy side of Japan, Inc., and what happens to outsiders trying to crowd in, but perhaps more importantly his case highlights shortcomings in Japan's judicial system. Drawing on a diary he kept in detention, he provides a detailed account of interrogations, browbeating, and the insistence that he implicate others in scenarios invented by the prosecutors. Based on this account, corroborated by many others treated similarly, one can understand how a detained person would eventually admit guilt and sign anything in order to win release. This helps explain why Japan's conviction rate is an alarming 99 percent; guilty until very rarely proven innocent. And what about the "bribed" politicians? None were ever prosecuted.


### Sagawa Kyubin Saga

In 1987 Takeshita Noboru was running for president of the LDP, a post that would make him Japan's new prime minister if he prevailed. He had many advantages having taken over Tanaka's political faction, the largest in the LDP, but at a series of fundraising events in Tokyo he was dogged by ultranationalists in vans bedecked with wartime rising sun flags and loudspeakers they used to heap effusive praise on him, proclaiming their support for his candidacy. This campaign of *homegoroshi* (embarrass through excessive praise) from a group Takeshita did not want such public backing from called for unorthodox countermeasures. Kanemaru Shin, a LDP heavyweight and Takeshita fixer, sought out Watanabe Hiroyasu, the president of the Sagawa Kyubin delivery firm and asked for his help. Watanabe's close ties to Ishii Susumu, head of the Inukai yakuza group, were well known and he arranged a meeting. Following that meeting, the vans disappeared and Takeshita became prime minister, one who was indebted to the mob.

In 1992, the Sagawa Kyubin scandal broke, revealing that this major delivery and trucking firm had distributed massive sums of cash to officials and politicians. Following on the heels of the Recruit scandal, corruption of such magnitude reinforced negative perceptions of politicians and left many Japanese disgusted with politics. Apparently, the cost of doing business in the developmental state was high. Kanemaru, former aide to Tanaka, had not reported a $4 million donation from Sagawa for which he was fined less than $2,000, prompting his resignation from politics under a cloud. At the time, he was the nation's kingmaker, party bagman, and backroom fixer, handpicking prime ministers and sponsoring politicians on the rise. A 1993 raid on his home and office unearthed a hidden trove of undeclared personal assets, including hundreds of pounds of gold bars, and some $50 million in currency and securities. In his files, investigators found detailed lists of undeclared donations from construction companies seeking public works contracts, which sparked a public furor about money politics that lead to the ouster of the LDP from power in 1993 for the first time since it was established in 1955. The Sagawa case was significant not only because the amounts were so large and the influence peddling by a top politician for personal enrichment so blatant, but also because the case linked the yakuza to Japan, Inc.

The overall state of Japanese democracy remains grim, as the LDP has thoroughly dominated what is effectively a one party state.[16] Voters briefly "threw the bums out" in 1993 and 2009, but the LDP has re-established its dominance despite scandals and flawed policies because there does not appear to be any viable opposition that gives them an alternative.[17] This lack of party competition is one key reason why almost half of eligible voters don't bother voting, opting out of a moribund and compromised democracy.

## Corporate Governance

The litany of shady practices associated with Japan, Inc. detailed above raises serious questions about the judgment and ethics of those in power. Such doubts have intensified as Japan, Inc. has been rocked by a series of high-profile scandals in recent years, including revelations that Olympus and Toshiba were cooking the books to hide massive losses. In the auto industry, Takata tried covering up its deadly airbags, Mitsubishi and Suzuki fiddled fuel efficiency data, Nissan and Subaru faked vehicle inspections, Honda, Mazda and Mitsubishi fudged diesel engine emissions, and Toyota was forced into extensive recalls due to various defects. And Kobe Steel admitted fabricating data for a decade regarding the durability and strength of its copper and aluminum products as workers felt pressure to produce good results and boost sales. Brand Japan has suffered from these revelations about management lapses, raising questions about quality and safety in a country renowned for its manufacturing prowess, pride in craftsmanship (*monozukuri*), work ethos, and honesty. The quality culture in Japan has eroded due to corner cutting and the globalization of supply chains that requires producers to do more for less. While these damning revelations of corporate cupidity and shoddy practices might be just the tip of the iceberg, they also suggest that corporate governance is slowly improving, as such dubious practices aren't all that new, but are now coming to light. In terms of Japan's third transformation, perhaps these cases are not the most inspiring examples of evolving norms and greater accountability, but do illustrate how what was once tolerated no longer passes muster, gets exposed, and is penalized.

Clearly, restoring credibility depends on improving corporate governance, something Prime Minister Abe Shinzo has championed with mixed results.

## *Cronyism*

In 2017 Abe was implicated in two scandals involving private schools and his cronies. The Moritomo Gakuen affair involved the sale of public land near Osaka at a whopping 86 percent discount to an associate of Abe who had pledged to name the private elementary school devoted to patriotic education in honor of the prime minister. He also received a grant to clean up industrial waste buried at the site that covered nearly the entire amount paid for the land, so essentially he got it for free. Apparently, local officials responsible for this sweetheart deal were acting on *sontaku* (an ingratiating, pre-emptive carrying out of an order that has not been given) in the belief that the prime minister's office supported the endeavor. Abe denied involvement and the local officials claimed they shredded the relevant documents that might have shed light on any improprieties. Related documents were not destroyed, however, and when subsequently divulged several months later, raised questions about bureaucratic complicity in a cover-up to protect Abe. In 2018 the scandal intensified after revelations that the original Ministry of Finance documents were altered. Comments by officials regarding the land deal in the original documents had cited the names of Abe, his wife, and other high-level LDP lawmakers who belonged to Nippon Kaigi (Japan Conference), an influential rightwing lobby organization known for its support of traditional values and patriotism. But their names were redacted from the documents submitted to the Diet in an attempt to exonerate Abe, but this backfired.

Another scandal that engulfed Abe broke in the summer of 2017 involving a similar pandering to authority. One of Abe's close friends sought special permission to open a veterinary school, but the government had not approved the opening of any new veterinary schools for half a century and there is no pressing need for another. But Kake Kotaro is a crony of Abe and it appears that officials took extraordinary measures to ensure his application would gain approval. The Kake scandal also involved *sontaku*, officials acting on the presumed intent of the prime minister, not his overt intervention. Officials testified in the Diet, however, about how a close aide of the prime minister did express support for the application, one of many factors that drove Abe's public support rate below 30 percent in July 2017. But in October he led the LDP to a resounding election victory and appeared to put the scandals behind him. In the 2018 Diet session, however, revelations of doctored data, document tampering and cover-ups linked to Abe reinforced widespread misgivings about his character, and polls indicated that 80% of the public did not believe his explanations about the scandals and cover-ups.

The third transformation of good governance, transparency, and accountability is exposing an entrenched conservative elite, one that is losing in the court of public opinion even as it retains the reins of power. As we shall see in the next chapter, this contested transformation is also manifest in national security.

# 3

# American Alliance

*Shin Godzilla* (2016), the 29th installment of this popular movie franchise, was a blockbuster, attracting throngs of Japanese to the spectacle of Tokyo's decimation by the notorious monster. The first Godzilla film in 1954 was released in the wake of a US hydrogen bomb test in the Bikini Atoll in the Pacific Ocean that released lethal levels of radioactive fallout that rendered the atoll uninhabitable. A Japanese fishing vessel, the Lucky Dragon, was located downwind of the testing site, and due to heavy exposure the crew fell ill with radiation sickness and one member died. This incident, less than a decade after the atomic bombings of Hiroshima and Nagasaki, drew extensive media coverage in Japan with considerable criticism of US carelessness and denials in addition to the impact on food safety; the catch of fish was contaminated, but brought back and sold in the market. The director acknowledges the inspiration from the public outcry as Godzilla was released from the seabed by the H-bomb test and stomped through Tokyo, wreaking destruction and contaminating the metropolis with his atomic fire breath. For Japanese audiences, the US was clearly implicated in the birth of Godzilla, his destructive powers, and the devastation he wrought in Japan.

Just as the 1954 atomic bomb test loomed over the launch of the Godzilla film series, the 2016 US presidential campaign waged by Donald Trump provided a troubling backdrop for many Japanese. Trump suggested it would be in the US interest if Japan developed nuclear weapons, while insisting that Japan would have to pay more to host US bases. Due to his erratic nature, Trump also sowed doubts about how committed the US was to its alliance with Japan. His open rejection of the Trans Pacific Partnership (TPP) was seen to augur US withdrawal from the region, ceding American influence to China. Since Abe had committed to TPP mostly out of geopolitical considerations and a desire to keep the US engaged as a counterweight to China, Trump's repudiation of the accord was viewed as a troubling sign just at a time when Japan felt threatened by an increasingly assertive China and North Korea's nuclear weapons program.

In 2016 Godzilla again laid waste to Tokyo's skyline, but the Japanese response to this crisis highlighted the virtues of teamwork and the need for more resolute leaders, presumably in the mold of Abe. The film was interpreted in some quarters as making strong political statements favoring Japan shedding Article 9, conferring new emergency powers on the prime minister, repudiating pacifism, and getting out from under the US thumb. The US comes across as an overbearing, self-seeking ally that puts its own interests ahead of Japan's, threatening a nuclear attack on Tokyo to kill Godzilla in order to protect the US.

So, if the US is not a reliable ally and willing to sacrifice Japan for its own interests, what can Tokyo do? The film suggests greater autonomy and relying on Japan's technological ingenuity, social cohesion, teamwork, indomitable spirit, and military power. Godzilla captures the zeitgeist of some segments of contemporary Japan, where President Trump's "America First" policy has amplified existing anxieties about relying on the US. The film makes a visceral case that Japan must overcome bureaucratic inertia and a feeble leadership to deal with an existential crisis. It is the Self-Defense Forces (SDF) and younger, patriotic Japanese, with help from France, who save the nation from their elders, the US, and Godzilla. While the film does not deliver an explicit endorsement of constitutional revision, it certainly implies pacifism is a luxury Japan can ill-afford and makes a powerful case for abandoning the indecisive, "pass the buck" mentality that prevails among a feckless and sclerotic governing elite.

In October 2017, Trump visited Abe in Japan in a show of solidarity aimed at North Korea and China. While golfing together, Abe yanked his shot into a deep bunker, but managed to hit his next shot onto the fairway without any trouble. But, as Abe climbed to the top of the bunker, he suddenly tumbled head over heels backward to the bottom, an undignified moment he probably did not want to go viral on the Internet. The video also showed that in this moment of distress, Trump was oblivious and strode down the fairway, leaving Abe all alone. This scene played to Japanese anxieties about the risks of cozying up to Trump, the least popular US president among Japanese since the alliance began in 1952. It is striking that Japanese confidence in US foreign policy plunged from nearly 80 percent under Barack Obama to 24 percent under Trump, and that poll was taken before his unsettling "fire and fury" rhetoric targeting North Korea.[1]

## Unequals

Japan has an unequal relationship with the US and, in matters of foreign and security policies, usually defers to and takes cues from Washington. The term client state is often invoked to highlight this subordinate relationship and the implications of an alliance that requires Japan to follow the US lead.[2] Across the ideological spectrum there is consensus that Japan has limited autonomy and is constrained in its diplomatic initiatives, but there is disagreement about whether this subordinate relationship is beneficial and indispensable to Japan. In general, conservatives see the alliance as essential and the only option for safeguarding Japan's security in an increasingly dangerous region, where North Korea and China threaten, while progressives assert it encroaches on national sovereignty, contravenes the constitution, subverts democratic values, accentuates regional tensions and endangers Japan because US bases are targets.

The disproportionate base-hosting burden for

Okinawa, where most US troops are based and military facilities are located, covering some 17 percent of the islands' total land area, has become intensely politicized. This military presence defies the democratic will of Okinawans who increasingly want the American bases relocated and downsized.

Strong anti-base sentiments draw on the collective trauma of war that is taught in schools, commemorated in museums and anniversaries and passed down in families from the older generation that experienced the devastating 1945 Battle of Okinawa. Aside from nearly 100,000 soldiers and local conscripts, an additional 100,000 Okinawan civilians died in that conflagration, about one quarter of the population, and resentments still simmer based on the knowledge that Tokyo used the islands as a sacrificial pawn at a time when the war was clearly lost. The sense of betrayal is reinforced by the Japanese government's agreement to allow the American military to maintain administrative control over the islands even after the US Occupation ended in 1952 while the rest of Japan regained independence. Okinawans had to wait until 1972 to join them.[3] From their perspective, Tokyo and Washington are disregarding their democratic voice expressed in numerous elections where anti-base candidates are elected, and thus ignoring one of the crucial shared values that underpin the alliance; yet again Okinawa is being used as a sacrificial pawn that marginalizes islanders' interests.[4]

The mainstream consensus positions the alliance

as vital to Japan and its subordination is just how things work given geopolitical realities. The Cold War between the Soviet Union and the US defined the international order from 1947 to 1989, and influenced the US Occupation of Japan and lingering military presence. The US embraced much of the wartime conservative elite, presiding over extensive continuities even while reinventing Japan.[5] The 1947 Constitution symbolized this transformation and US emphasis on demilitarizing and democratizing Japan. By imposing unilateral pacifism on Japan through Article 9, the US assumed responsibility for protecting its protege while war-weary Japanese welcomed this and other reforms. This US security role defined the subordinate bilateral relationship, but Tokyo's elite were mostly willing minions, focusing instead on economic recovery from war devastation. Japan's weakness dictated its options and highlighted the benefits of the US security umbrella, in addition to unimpeded access to the US market and cutting-edge technologies. From this perspective, Washington's extensive support more than offset the inherent inequality in relations. Certainly, Japanese political and business leaders rankled at the American harangues and arm-twisting that was sometimes involved, but they also developed the art of managing the ally and securing access to the corridors of Washington power to influence policies. Thus, the puppet state argument fails to capture the dynamic interactions of the relationship, and the ways that Japan, Inc. could at times play its hand to advance national interests despite the US holding most of the trump cards. Okinawa's lingering trauma is a cost that most Japanese are prepared to endure because they are unaffected by this distant suffering.

### Remaking Japan

During the Occupation (1945–52), US General Douglas MacArthur enacted policies aimed at reinventing Japan as a pacifist democracy. This included demobilization of the military and purges of militarists from government ministries and politics. The 1947 Constitution was written by the US to promote a comprehensive democratization of Japan by de-concentrating power, establishing institutional checks and balances, and promoting civil liberties. Believing that the excessive concentration of power under the Meiji Constitution played a major role in the militarists derailing democracy in the 1930s and leading Japan into war, the Americans produced a new set of ground rules for the Japanese polity that were designed to ensure that the US would not have to fight another Pacific War two decades hence, as was the case with Germany following WWI.

The war-renouncing Article 9 prohibited Japan from rearming. This establishment of a pacifist state was warmly embraced by a public that rightly blamed militarists for all they suffered due to a reckless bid to subjugate Asia between 1931 and 1945. Citizens also welcomed democratization that empowered unions, guaranteed a free press, freedom of assembly and speech, and diluted the power of the central government, especially the once dreaded police. They also welcomed curtailment of the Ministry of Education's powers because it had nurtured blind devotion to the Emperor and jingoistic beliefs in the innate superiority of the Japanese people that facilitated wartime militarism.

Other developments in 1947 ensured it was a pivotal year in the remaking of Japan. The Cold War with the Soviet Union erupted and transformed US objectives in Japan. Demilitarizing and democratizing Japan, and holding warmongering militarists accountable for their "crimes against peace," gave way to efforts to remake Japan into a reliable ally, both militarily and ideologically. US bases in Japan became the teeth in the new containment policy outlined by George Kennan aimed at stopping the spread of communism by projecting US military power in Asia. Also, in 1947, the US initiated a "red purge" of several thousand journalists, union organizers, and others deemed to have communist sympathies. The International Military Tribunal for the Far East (IMFTE) known as the Tokyo Trials (1946–8), established to hold top-level leaders accountable for initiating the war and to inform the Japanese public about the horrors inflicted on Asia, was quickly wound down. The IMFTE was marred by a deeply flawed judicial process, often referred to as "victor's justice," that ensured the convictions of 26

Class A war crimes suspects and the hanging of seven of them.[6] But others question this judicial lynching narrative and stress the proceedings were valuable for documenting Japanese war crimes.[7] The onset of the Cold War, however, dampened American enthusiasm for pursuing justice. An additional 43 Class A war crimes suspects, including future Prime Minister Kishi Nobusuke, Abe's grandfather, were never put on trial, as priorities shifted from retribution toward rehabilitating Japan and embracing it as an ally.

## San Francisco System

The US Occupation ended in 1952 after the signing of the San Francisco Peace Treaty and a bilateral security treaty in 1951. The resulting security alliance with the US, and the complicated legacies of this treaty, continue to shape the geopolitical landscape of Asia.[8] At San Francisco, the US established a Cold War order in Asia that has persisted beyond the collapse of the Soviet Union. These treaties were negotiated while Japan was occupied amid a spiraling Cold War frenzy, spiking in 1949 due to Mao Zedong's communists prevailing in China's civil war and the Soviet Union's first atomic bomb test. In 1950, the announcement of Beijing and Moscow's alliance further stoked anxieties in Washington, especially after the midyear outbreak of the Korean War (1950–3). Ominous developments in Indochina where Ho Chi Minh's communists were resisting French efforts to restore colonial rule fueled

hysteria in Washington about Moscow's machina-
tions, suspicions reinforced by China's entry into the
Korean War.

The San Francisco system profoundly influenced
Japan's foreign relations in Asia in the post-WWII
era.[9] With US backing, Japan was reintegrated into
the region on Washington's terms and in support of
its Cold War agenda. This agenda was defined by
rivalry with the Soviet Union/China and the US policy
of containment targeting the spread of communism.
The 1951 US–Japan security treaty established an
alliance with the US that required Japan to host US
military bases. The treaty brought an end to the US
Occupation, restoring Japanese independence with
the exception of Okinawa where US bases were (and
are) concentrated. As noted above, this strategically
located island chain remained a US satrapy until 1972.

The other pillar of the San Francisco System is the
Treaty of Peace, an agreement signed by 48 allied
nations. Japan was stripped of its former colonies and
possessions and agreed to pay reparations and compensation. Key governments did not sign the treaty,
including the Soviet Union, Communist China and
Nationalist China (governed by the Kuomintang
based in Taiwan), and South and North Korea. The
absence of these prominent belligerents and former
colonies sowed seeds of discord between Japan and
neighboring nations, leaving a legacy of prolonged
estrangement in northeast Asia that persists in the
twenty-first century.

The exclusion of China from the peace conference deepened a rift that postponed reconciliation with the nation that suffered most from Japanese aggression. Washington further complicated this situation by pressuring Japan to sign a peace treaty in 1952 with the Republic of China (ROC) in Taiwan, forcing Tokyo to join the US in recognizing the ROC as the legitimate government of China rather than the People's Republic of China (PRC) that controlled all of mainland China. Japanese officials and businessmen had misgivings about US insistence on isolating China while pretending that Taiwan was the legitimate power, but ending the US occupation and regaining sovereignty was the government's priority.[10] This state of affairs persisted until 1972 when Tokyo followed Washington's abrupt shift and normalized relations with the PRC, followed in 1978 by a Treaty of Peace and Friendship. The evolution of Japan's relationship with China is a good example of the client state relationship, as Tokyo dutifully adjusted to the sudden normalization without any prior consultation, swallowing its loss of face and resentment as a vassal must do.

Given that the Korean War was ongoing during negotiations for the Treaty of Peace, there was some logic to excluding representatives from the Korean peninsula, but this also delayed a reckoning over the oppression and indignities suffered by the Korean people under Japanese colonial rule between 1910 and 1945. The Soviet Union attended the peace conference, but did not sign the treaty because it objected to the exclusion of China and Washington's agenda of enlisting Japan as an ally in the Cold War targeting Moscow. It further complained that it had not been properly consulted in the drafting of the treaty and objected to the denial of China's rights to Taiwan. It welcomed Japan's renunciation of all claims to the Kuril Islands, but condemned the treaty's failure to recognize Soviet sovereignty over South Sakhalin and the Kuril Islands as promised in the Yalta Agreement of February 1945, leaving their disposition unsettled.[11]

The PRC was not invited and denounced the treaty as illegal and did not recognize it. Beijing also objected to the treaty's failure to recognize Chinese claims to Taiwan, as well as the Paracel, Pratas and Spratly Islands in the South China Sea, issues that have become increasingly tendentious in the twenty-first century. The treaty is ambiguous about Taiwan's status because it is not ceded to any nation, although it required Japan to renounce its sovereignty. China maintains that Japan accepted the Instrument of Surrender based on the terms of the Potsdam Declaration and thus Taiwan should revert to Beijing. This is because the 1945 Potsdam Declaration incorporates the Cairo Declaration of 1943, in which the Allied powers agreed to retrocession of sovereignty over any territory gained as spoils of war as was the case with Japan gaining Taiwan as a colony following the Sino–Japanese War of 1894–5.

## *Disputed Territories*

At San Francisco, the US sowed the seeds of contemporary territorial disputes between Japan, Russia,
China (Taiwan), and South Korea. The settlement did
not clarify sovereignty over three sets of islands that
put Japan at odds with its neighbors. The disputed
islands are known differently by the rival claimants:

1. the Kuriles (Russia)/Northern Territories (Japan)
   north of Hokkaido;
2. Dokdo (South Korea)/Takeshima (Japan) in the Sea
   of Japan/East Sea between South Korea and Japan
   that are sometimes called the Liancourt Rocks; and
3. the Senkaku (Japan)/Diaoyu(China)/Diaoyutai
   (Taiwan) in the East China Sea between Okinawa
   and Taiwan that are sometimes called the Pinnacle
   Islands.

These disputed islands rouse nationalist passions and
are a source of bitter recriminations and diplomatic
deadlock. The importance of these islands increased
with the 1982 United Nations Convention on the
Law of the Sea (UNCLOS). In establishing the right
to claim territorial waters extending 12 nautical miles
from the coast, and Exclusive Economic Zones (EEZ)
extending 200 nautical miles from the baseline of territorial waters, the economic significance of islands
increased dramatically. Rich fisheries and the potential for natural gas and seabed minerals raised the

stakes for all the disputants. Each has established a legal basis backing up their claims based on treaties, agreements, documents, maps, and history that are hotly contested. Suffice to say that Japan insists that its claims should prevail and the government has instructed textbook publishers to clarify that these islands are inherent territory and in 2018 opened up a museum where Tokyo's claims to Takeshima and the Senkaku are presented. This curatorial salvo was greeted with a chorus of protests from Beijing, Seoul, and Taipei.

In 2005, the Japanese prefecture of Shimane declared February 22 to be Takeshima Day, attracting small crowds of ultranationalists, some of whom ride around on black buses spewing invective and patriotic songs from the wartime era over loudspeakers. Angry Korean demonstrators outside the Japanese Embassy in Seoul protest Japan's claim, sometimes by severing fingers and throwing rocks. In 2012, during the London Olympics, a South Korean football player was barred from the medal podium for celebrating victory over Japan by displaying a placard: "Dokdo is our territory." The government took the unusual step of rewarding him for his patriotic gesture by exempting him from military service. Not long after, President Lee Myung Bak became the first sitting South Korean president to set foot on Dokdo in a bid to bolster his sinking poll numbers, sending bilateral relations into a tailspin.

The Senkaku islands, uninhabited rocky outcrops

in the East China Sea between Taiwan and Okinawa, have sparked tensions between Beijing and Tokyo that have escalated considerably since 2010.[12] Japan exercises administrative control over the Senkaku while China has been increasingly assertive about its Diaoyu claims with frequent sorties of vessels and planes into the sea and airspace claimed by Japan. In response, Japan has increased coastguard patrols and scrambles by jets to warn off the Chinese "intruders." This militarization of the dispute creates a dangerous flashpoint in Asia, where miscalculation or overreaction could spark conflict.

Aside from the rival legal claims, Beijing maintains that in 1972, when Japanese Prime Minister Tanaka Kakuei and Chinese Premier Zhou Enlai met in Beijing to normalize diplomatic relations, and again in 1978 when Japanese Foreign Minister Sunoda Sunao met with Vice Premier Deng Xiaoping, the question of the Senkaku islands was discussed. China claims that the leaders agreed to shelve the question of sovereignty for future resolution, while leaving the islands under Japanese administration. The Japanese government maintains that there was no such agreement, although a prominent confidante of Tanaka, LDP heavyweight Nonaka Hirofumi, caused a stir in mid-2012 when he announced that Tanaka had told him there was. The British archives also confirm that in 1982 Prime Minister Suzuki Zenko told Margaret Thatcher about the Japanese government's policy of shelving the sovereignty dispute.

In 1972, with the reversion of Okinawa to Japanese sovereignty, the Senkaku were placed under Japanese administration and thus under the ambit of the US–Japan security treaty.[13] But the US State Department made clear that this move did not prejudice underlying claims to sovereignty. China and Taiwan asserted sovereignty over the islands for the first time in 1971.

In 2010, the Japanese Coast Guard arrested the crew of a Chinese fishing boat that rammed one of its vessels near the Senkaku. This sparked a major diplomatic row, violent anti-Japanese demonstrations across China, and a virtual ban on rare earth metal exports from China to Japan, a vital material in various high-tech products. The Chinese crew and captain were released, but the islets became a focus of rising anti-Japanese animosity and an unlikely touchstone of national identity. In 2012, Japan purchased three of the five islands from their private Japanese owner, effectively nationalizing them. This further soured relations with China, stirring anxieties among Japanese voters and propelling the hawkish Abe Shinzo and his LDP back into power a few months later.

The Northern Territories refers to four disputed islands – Kunashiri, Etorofu, Habomai, and Shikotan. The Soviet Union invaded and seized these islands at the end of WWII, after Japan announced its surrender on August 15, 1945. From the Japanese perspective, Soviet and now Russian claims are therefore illegal. Since 1981, February 7 is celebrated in Japan as Northern Territories Day, a reminder of the anniversary of the 1855 treaty with Russia that recognized Japanese claims to the islands.

Moscow views its claim as justified because in February 1945 Soviet leader Joseph Stalin met with US President Franklin Roosevelt and British Prime Minister Winston Churchill at Yalta, making various concessions in exchange for Soviet help in defeating Japan. As agreed at Yalta, Stalin launched his attack on August 9, 1945, three months after Germany's surrender, mounting a successful blitzkrieg through Japan's depleted defenses in Manchuria and Korea. The Soviet forces continued fighting and seized the disputed islands by September 1945.

In the 1951 Treaty of San Francisco Japan specifically, "renounces all right, title and claim to the Kurile Islands, and to that portion of Sakhalin and the islands adjacent to it over which Japan acquired sovereignty as a consequence of the Treaty of Portsmouth of 5 September 1905." Although Moscow never signed the Treaty of San Francisco, it takes this renunciation as endorsement of its claim. Japan insists that the four islands are not actually part of the Kuriles and thus they were not renounced. Back in 1956, Tokyo and Moscow were on the verge of resolving the impasse by splitting the four islands, but the US pressured Japan not to strike a deal with the common Cold War enemy. As a result, bilateral relations have remained chilly despite several Japanese overtures. Under General Secretary Mikhail Gorbachev, during the final years of the Soviet Union at the end of the 1980s, Japanese hopes for a breakthrough rested on Moscow's need for economic assistance. Gorbachev's political weakness and the strategically valuable location of the islands, however, precluded any territorial concessions.

Since 2013 Prime Minister Abe has vigorously pursued a settlement of the island dispute, frequently meeting with Russian President Vladimir Putin despite US-led sanctions and international isolation following Russia's seizure of the Crimea in 2014. This is a rare example of Japan pursuing diplomacy in defiance of US preferences, but Abe's efforts have not swayed Moscow. On a brief visit to Japan at the end of 2016, Putin dampened any hopes of a deal on the islands. They have strategic importance for Russia's Far East submarine fleet operating in the Sea of Okhotsk and control access to the Pacific. Moreover, the Abe government refused to rule out the possibility that the US could station military assets on the islands should Japan regain control. This is unacceptable to Moscow and militates against retrocession of any of the islands. Russia's subsequent installation of missile batteries on two of the islands, and the 2018 announcement that warplanes would be deployed and a new naval base constructed there, are part of a rapid military build-up that reinforces doubts Moscow will compromise in this dispute.

## Yoshida Doctrine

This was the most important pillar of Japanese security policy in the postwar period, one that caused tensions in the US–Japan alliance because Washington sought a greater military contribution from Tokyo. Prime Minister Yoshida emphasized economic recovery and invoked the war-renouncing Article 9 in the US-written 1947 Constitution to ward off US demands that Japan remilitarize and participate in the American-led United Nations war effort in the Korean Peninsula (1950–3). The US quickly came to regret this provision that it had insisted on, while Yoshida found it convenient. He did, however, authorize the creation of a National Police Reserve in 1950 with 75,000 reservists to cope with internal threats and natural disasters that was expanded and became the basis for the 1954 establishment of Japan's Self-Defense Forces.[14]

There seems to be little ambiguity or scope in Article 9 for Japan to rearm as it incrementally did in the postwar era. However, Japanese courts have upheld the government's position that defensive military forces are not banned by Article 9, and proponents also argue that all nations retain the right to self-defense as specified by the UN Charter.[15] Tokyo stonewalled persistent US pressures to rearm during the tense atmosphere of the Cold War, but gradually and incrementally acceded to US demands for greater burden sharing on defense to ward off accusations it was free riding at American expense. The minimalist approach to security embodied in the Yoshida Doctrine – doing the minimum required to assuage Washington – sought to dampen domestic controversies over security issues. In 1960 there were mass protests against the revised Treaty of Mutual Cooperation and Security between the US and Japan that brought down the government, but only after Prime Minister Kishi managed to get it passed in the Diet. His ignominious ouster demonstrated the popularity of pacifism in Japan, drawing on widespread public repudiation of militarists like Kishi and the debacle they inflicted on the nation and region.

In the context of the Cold War, Japan was a shining example that contrasted with miserable conditions in the Soviet Union's orbit of influence. By hosting US military bases, Japan also played a crucial role in the US war effort in Korea and later Vietnam, in the latter case sparking widespread protests and a radicalized leftist student movement that targeted US imperialism and Tokyo's "betrayal" of fellow Asians. It is often argued that the continued presence of many US military bases more than seven decades after the occupation ended is a sign of Japan's subordination to the US. Even though the 1947 Constitution seems to limit the Japanese government's security options, it never affected its willingness to accommodate US demands for base privileges, nor, it appears, constrain repeated US violations of Japan's Three Non-Nuclear Principles. These violations highlight the nature of Japan's client state status.

Prime Minister Sato Eisaku (1964–72) first enunciated Japan's Three Non-Nuclear Principles in 1967. These prohibit the production, possession, or introduction of nuclear weapons into Japanese territory. In 1974 he won the Nobel Peace Prize for doing so, but it was subsequently revealed that he was aware of repeated US violations of these principles. There was a secret agreement between Japan and the US that allowed US nuclear weapons into Japanese territory that was concluded when the US–Japan security treaty was revised in 1960, acquiescing to US ships carrying nuclear weapons to transit Japanese waters and call at Japanese ports. There also was a similar secret agreement allowing the US to bring nuclear weapons into Okinawa in a crisis, and some were actually stored there prior to reversion in 1972.

Overall, the Yoshida Doctrine constrained what Japan was prepared to do in support of the US militarily, but over the decades US pressure on Tokyo led to incremental changes. From 1978, for example, Tokyo began paying base-hosting support that defrayed the costs of stationing US troops in Japan. And, in the 1980s, Prime Minister Nakasone Yasuhiro (1981–6) agreed to expand the surrounding maritime area that Japan would defend and boldly declared that the nation was an "unsinkable aircraft carrier," shrugging off pacifist criticisms.

As Japan became the second largest economy in the world, there were rising expectations overseas, and among some Japanese, that it would play a more prominent role in the world. Yoshida's emphasis on economic growth had borne fruit in ways that catapulted Japan into the global limelight and whet

ambitions for normalizing its security policy. It would
not be until the 1990s, however, that Japan began to
discuss a "normal nation" security policy, one that
posited Japan should play a role on the global stage
commensurate with its economic heft and interests.[16]
This was prompted by concerns that Japan had only
contributed money toward the Persian Gulf War
(1990–1) and was vulnerable to criticism that it was
shirking risk while enjoying the benefits of continued access to Middle East oil. Subsequently, Japan
dispatched troops overseas for the first time in 1993
under a new Peacekeeping Operations law, and in
1997 agreed to new US–Japan Defense Guidelines
that expanded what Japan's SDF would do in the
region if the need arose. These represented significant
steps in the gradual loosening of constitutional constraints and taking on security tasks that stretched the
limits of the Yoshida Doctrine.[17]

### Korean Relations

The divisive legacies of Japanese colonial rule over the
Korean peninsula have bedeviled Japan's relations with
Seoul and Pyongyang since the end of WWII. Due to
the Cold War and Korean civil war (1951–3) when
Japan was used as a base for US military operations,
relations with North Korea were limited. Between
1959 and 1984, the International Committee of the
Red Cross repatriated nearly 100,000 ethnic Koreans
who were resident in Japan to North Korea, including

49,000 in 1960 alone. This mass repatriation resulted from negotiations between North Korea and Japan beginning in 1955, Tokyo's vigorous promotion of the exodus, and North Korean propaganda channeled through ideologically sympathetic organizations in Japan. Some repatriates also hoped to help their preferred homeland, a patriotic choice many suffered for, given grim conditions in North Korea.

Japanese airplane hijackers associated with the radical leftist Red Army found refuge in North Korea since the 1970s, meaning Pyongyang was harboring what Tokyo viewed as fugitives from justice. Finding them partners, along with identity theft and tutoring in Japanese, are some of the reasons why in the 1970s and 1980s North Korean commandoes abducted dozens of Japanese nationals from Japan and brought them back to North Korea.[18] Few observers believed scattered reports about this abduction program at the time, but President Kim Jong-il confirmed it in 2002 when he met Prime Minister Koizumi Junichiro in Pyongyang. Since then, bilateral relations have been frosty as Japan sought an account of what happened to the dozens of Japanese citizens Tokyo believes were abducted. Japan linked its participation in the Six Party Talks (2003–9), aimed at getting North Korea to end its nuclear weapons program, with a full accounting of the abductees' fate, but this has not been forthcoming. The escalating level of missile and nuclear weapon tests under Kim Jong-un (2012–) antagonizes and frightens Japan's residents, buttressing the mainstream consensus about the indispensability of the US security alliance.

In 1965, Japan normalized relations with South Korea through the Treaty on Basic Relations. This treaty came two decades after the end of Japanese colonial rule and at the behest of the US in order to enhance cooperation with and between its two regional allies. The treaty provided for compensation by Japan to South Korea intended to resolve all issues and claims arising from Japanese colonial rule. Tokyo disbursed $500 million in loans and granted $300 million in economic aid, money that jumpstarted South Korea's development of heavy industry and infrastructure.

In the decades following the 1965 Treaty, Japan–South Korea relations remained fraught. Indeed, historical conflicts surfaced repeatedly and have intensified since democratization of South Korea at the end of the 1980s. In 2005, the government of South Korea released diplomatic documents covering negotiations about the 1965 agreement that reveal Japan had proposed offering compensation directly to individuals, but Seoul took charge of such disbursements. Although accepting a large sum of Japanese compensation for a million Koreans conscripted as laborers or soldiers in exchange for waiving all future claims, the South Korean government paid victim families only modest sums of 300,000 won (approximately $1,200) for each death and spent most of the Japanese redress allocated for individual compensation on industrialization and infrastructure projects.

Ongoing recriminations over such issues suggest that the Treaty provided no substantial basis for overcoming the contentious colonial past or advancing reconciliation. From a South Korean perspective, the historical issues – notably the comfort women, forced laborers, and Japanese textbook treatments of colonialism and war – require unqualified Japanese recognition of wrongdoing, acceptance of responsibility, and compensation.

## Reconciliation Postponed

Due to the calculus of the Cold War, the US delayed Japan's regional reconciliation efforts, preferring to promote its ally as a paragon of pacifism and modernization rather than dwell on historical grievances. Washington prioritized containing communism and isolating China, forcing Japan to follow suit. Overall, Japan's postwar reconciliation efforts to improve relations with nations it invaded, occupied, and colonized pre-1945 have been much less successful in northeast Asia than southeast Asia. Japanese imperialism had a greater impact on China and the Korean Peninsula because it lasted longer and was more intrusive and destructive, trampling on the dignity of these nations and leaving deep scars. With the notable exception of Taiwan, the perception that Japan is not fully contrite about, or apologetic concerning, its colonial and wartime misdeeds hinders reconciliation. In the 1950s, with prodding from Washington, Japan signed reparation agreements with Burma, the Philippines, Indonesia, and South Vietnam. The amounts were relatively small, totaling just over $1 billion, and in the form of export credits that were tied to purchases of Japanese goods and services. This economic reintegration through reparations enabled Japanese firms to gain market share, but this generated a backlash by the 1970s. Anger about Japan's economic domination led Tokyo to proclaim the 1977 Fukuda Doctrine.[19] Prime Minister Fukuda Takeo (1976–8) declared that Japan would never become a military power, would nurture trust with southeast Asian countries, and promote peace and prosperity in the region. He also sought to offer reassurance in the wake of the US withdrawal from southeast Asia following defeat in the Vietnam War. These principles heralded a significant strengthening of cooperation between Japan and southeast Asian countries as Tokyo embraced what it called "heart-to-heart" diplomacy and promoted enhanced cultural and educational exchanges. Relations are not hostage to history, and Japan enjoys good relations throughout the region, is a major investor and trading partner, and plays a prominent role in ASEAN (Association of Southeast Asian Nations), the Asian Development Bank, and other regional organizations and forums. The contrast with northeast Asia is profound.

Tokyo's fractious relationship with Seoul is problematic for the US because it seeks more trilateral security cooperation with its allies. During the Obama Administration (2009–17), there was sustained pressure to enhance security cooperation and substantive progress with conclusion of an agreement on direct sharing of military intelligence in 2016. In 2012, domestic opposition to a similar accord led Seoul to abruptly withdraw approval, illustrating the vagaries of relations between "frenemies."

The 2016 intelligence sharing agreement was facilitated in part by a 2015 agreement to resolve the comfort women issue. Behind-the-scenes pressure from Washington pushed the two nations to overcome their differences over this system of sexual slavery that involved the recruitment of tens of thousands of Korean women in the 1930s and 1940s through deception and coercion at the behest of the Japanese military. The Japanese government agreed to pay 1 billion yen (about $9 million) to fund a Korean foundation that would distribute the funds to any of the then 46 surviving comfort women who would accept the money. Both governments also agreed to refrain from criticizing each other regarding this issue in the international community. Disagreement spiraled, however, over the continued presence of a comfort woman statue across from the Japanese Embassy in Seoul. The agreement doesn't actually require removal of the statue, but commits Seoul to trying to do so. Tokyo apparently sees the removal as an implicit quid pro quo for the money transferred and was livid when another similar statue was erected next to the Japanese consulate in Busan. As a result, Japan withdrew its ambassador for four months in 2017, as relations soured at a time when turmoil was peaking over the impeachment of President Park Geun-hye and intensification of North Korea's nuclear weapons and missile testing program.

In May 2017, newly elected President Moon Jae-in received a congratulatory phone call from Prime Minister Abe who lost no time in pressing Moon to abide by the 2015 agreement. Moon explained that the agreement had almost no public support and asked for patience. At the end of 2017, a South Korean task force charged with reviewing the agreement issued a negative verdict, pointing out that the negotiations were conducted in secret and there was no effort to consult victims or advocacy groups. The panel concluded that, "The Victim Centered Approach, which has been established as an international standard when it comes to the women's human rights during war, was not sufficiently reflected during the negotiation process." Adding, "It is difficult to resolve a historical issue such as the 'Comfort Women' issue by short term measures through diplomatic negotiation or political compromise." Nonetheless, Moon agreed to abide by the accord but called on Abe to offer a public apology. Japan rejected this request, insisting that the deal is "final and irreversible," yet it has only become yet another bone of contention.

Previous efforts to resolve the comfort women issue also failed. In the 1993 Kono Statement, the Japanese government acknowledged state responsibility for the coercive recruitment of comfort women and promised to make amends and teach about it. Between 1995 and 2007, the Asia Women's Fund (AWF) operated at the government's behest and was funded by private donors ($5 million) and the state ($31 million) to offer compensation. This included Dutch women, but altogether only 364 women received money and the total amount of solatia distributed amounted to just $19 million. The AWF contributed little to regional reconciliation and, like the 2015 comfort women accord, sparked recriminations that ensure the divisive past still looms large in the twenty-first century. Washington remains frustrated that enhanced security cooperation is being held hostage to history and that its allies are still battling over the past rather than cooperating to deal with contemporary security threats.

## *Third Rail*

Prime Minister Hatoyama Yukio (2009–10) and his Democratic Party of Japan (DPJ) won a landslide victory in the 2009 elections, ousting the LDP from power. He called for a review of the 2006 Roadmap negotiated between the US and Japan that was prompted by the gang rape of a 12-year-old schoolgirl in Okinawa by US servicemen in 1995. This roadmap was a plan to reduce the US military footprint in Okinawa that hinged on relocating the US marine airbase from a densely populated residential area in Futenma, Ginowan City, to Henoko, where construction is now underway on a new airfield in pristine Oura Bay. This plan has aroused sustained and intense local opposition on environmental grounds, and also because it remains unclear how building a new base is consistent with the Roadmap's goal of scaling back the US military presence.

Hatoyama's suggestion to review the Roadmap drew a harsh reaction from Washington, as did his call for establishing more balanced relations with the US and China. In terms of alliance politics, these were extremely provocative positions that questioned some basic assumptions of an alliance in which Japan as the junior partner is expected to defer on security matters.[20] US Defense Secretary Robert Gates visited Tokyo and read the government the riot act. While Hatoyama's initiatives did not threaten to sunder the alliance, and seemed more like an overdue effort to stop acting like a vassal state, it appeared that he stepped on the third rail. From Wikileaks we learned that bureaucrats in Japan's Ministry of Foreign Affairs colluded with American officials to discredit and undermine Hatoyama, a campaign that was very successful. His brief tenure was capsized by the relentless focus on his failed efforts to find any location outside Okinawa willing to host the Futenma replacement base. The domestic media was like a lynch mob demanding his head for weakening the alliance. The LDP, bureaucracy, and media also played a critical role in stonewalling Hatoyama's entire legislative agenda, contributing to his downfall. He certainly was not one of Japan's better leaders, proving more inept than inspired, and in taking on the Pentagon, he learned the hard way that Washington gets its way. Alliance managers are far more pleased with Prime Minister Abe, who has done more than all his predecessors combined to deliver on the Pentagon's longstanding wish list.

## *Abe Doctrine*

The Abe Doctrine, branded as "proactive pacifism," is incrementally replacing the Yoshida Doctrine of a minimalist security posture.[21] Through enhanced security ties with the US, reinterpretation of the Constitution, and sweeping new security legislation, Abe has steadily expanded what Japan is prepared to do militarily in support of the US. In doing so he has challenged longstanding pacifist norms and values. In 2017 he boldly promised to revise Article 9 of the Constitution by 2020, coinciding with the Tokyo Summer Olympics, saying "That will be a year when a newly reborn Japan begins to move strongly forward." However, the public does not share his enthusiasm.

The ink was barely dry on the 2015 US–Japan Defense Guidelines unveiled during Prime Minister Abe's April visit to Washington, DC, when Senator John McCain, chairman of the US Armed Services Committee, issued a wakeup call to the Japanese people. He said he expects Japan's SDF to put boots on the ground in the event of conflict on the Korean Peninsula and hopes it will scale up operations in the

Middle East and the South China Sea in support of US military forces. McCain's comments highlighted that the new guidelines expand considerably what Japan has committed to do in support of its US ally, shedding previous geographic constraints. The US, however, is far more enthusiastic about the new arrangements than the Japanese people.

A 2015 Pew Poll indicated that 23 percent of Japanese favor an expanded security role with 68 percent opposed, while a Jiji Press poll that year found only 14 percent support for the Abe Doctrine while NHK found a 22 percent support rate, underscoring the gaping chasm between public sentiments and the Tokyo–Washington security axis. Evidently, Japanese are concerned that the US will drag Japan into a war unrelated to Japan's direct security interests.

Abe seeks to add a proviso to Article 9 that would acknowledge the constitutionality of the SDF because he finds it deplorable that some constitutional scholars question this. Whether they recognize the SDF or not, however, nearly all of Japan's constitutional scholars believe Abe's 2015 collective self-defense (CSD) legislation is unconstitutional. During Diet deliberations about the CSD legislation, even the LDP's handpicked constitutional scholars raised such doubts, awkward testimony that did not deter Abe.

In securing passage of the CSD legislation, Abe agreed to three vague principles that ostensibly constrain Japan's military actions. These principles grant the prime minister considerable discretionary authority to deploy the military if he/she alone determines that:

1. Japan or a country closely related with Japan is under military attack, which poses a threat to Japan's existence and puts Japanese nationals' lives, freedom, and their right to pursuit of happiness in clear danger;
2. there are no other means to overcome the above-mentioned danger so as to ensure the existence of Japan and the protection of Japanese nationals; and
3. the military engagement is limited to the minimum necessary use of force.

Polls showing persistently high opposition to the CSD legislation suggest the public is not reassured by these malleable constraints.

The CSD legislation passed in September 2015 provides a legal foundation for Japan to deliver on what it already promised in signing the new defense guidelines in Washington.[22] Abe committed the government to an expanded security role before securing Diet approval, creating an unfortunate impression that catering to Washington's concerns took precedence over heeding the will of the Japanese people. This legislation is at the heart of the Abe Doctrine, aimed at unleashing the Japanese military from longstanding constitutional constraints. This significant shift in security policy is driven by anxieties over China's

regional hegemonic ambitions and increasing assertiveness about its territorial claims.

Japan's greatest geopolitical dilemma is how to
cope with China's growing power and assertiveness,
most dramatically illustrated by the ongoing dispute
involving rival claims to the Senkaku/Diaoyu islands
in the East China Sea. Despite the apparent guaran-
tees in the Japan–US security treaty, and Washington's
repeated reassurances that it applies to the Senkaku
islands, Tokyo is not fully reassured by Article 5:

> Each Party recognizes that an armed attack against
> either Party in the territories under the administra-
> tion of Japan would be dangerous to its own peace
> and safety and declares that it would act to meet the
> common danger in accordance with its constitutional
> provisions and processes.

The intent is clear, but the wording does not specify
how the US might act or respond. One side's deliberate strategic ambiguity is another's source of anxiety.
Tokyo's abiding fear is that the US just might decide
not to jeopardize relations with China over some
uninhabited remote rocks in the East China Sea. So
even if it seems certain that the US would respond as
Tokyo wishes, a gnawing angst lingers.

To some extent the Pentagon and Japanese hawks
are hyping the China threat to help push agendas,
but Beijing is not helping matters with its clumsy
diplomacy, brinksmanship, and sweeping maritime

territorial claims backed by saber rattling and land reclamation projects in the Spratly Islands located over 1,000 km from China's coast. It has also antagonized the US and Japan by not doing more to rein in North Korea and propping it up economically.

Certainly, the rise of China requires some degree of strategic accommodation, but on what terms? Perhaps a combination of deterrence and mutual economic interests will avert conflict between China and the US/Japan, reinforced by shared global interests, but China is an ambitious power and history is not littered with examples of status quo powers conceding enough to coopt rising powers and avert conflict. Japan knows this story all too well from its own misadventures during the 1930s and 1940s. Thus, the Abe Doctrine seems more like a stopgap tactic rather than a compelling strategic vision. Détente with China is imperative, and there are some encouraging signs, but the hard work of diplomacy lies ahead. Meanwhile Japan faces other problems, notably the prolonged malaise of the Lost Decades that we examine in the next chapter.

# 4

# Lost Decades and Disasters

The story of Japan's Lost Decades began in the early 1990s, but the economic malaise persisted into the twenty-first century. Prime Minister Abe Shinzo promoted Abenomics to end that stagnation, and there are positive signs of progress in doing so, but after many false dawns over the years and the dilemmas posed by a shrinking and aging population, the public remains skeptical.

The collapse of the late 1980s asset bubble precipitated the Lost Decades, as stock and land prices imploded by over 60 percent, burying banks under bad loans and forcing investors into staggering losses. The exuberance and hubris of the 1980s gave way to gathering anxieties that extended beyond the state of the economy. Two major events in 1995 – the Kobe earthquake and a terrorist attack by Aum Shinrikyo, a religious cult – reinforced public perceptions that the government was ineffectual, generating a sense of crisis and despair about a system that was no longer capable of dealing with the challenges confronting Japan. This vanishing confidence also drew on a series of scandals implicating the mandarins and politicians who were the guardians of the Japan, Inc., post-WWII model; they and that system lost credibility. These changing perceptions and ebbing support for a system that had worked quite well for four decades is propelling Japan's slow-motion third transformation; it is so gradual and incremental there are reasons to doubt it is even happening. Yet, the ways and means of that model are now questioned. A frustrated public is no longer as deferential, and desperate for those in charge to offer a vision of hope and get on with the job.

People understand that the bureaucrats who guided the economic miracle made a series of mistakes that led to the Lost Decades and also in dealing with the consequences. This was exacerbated by a fusty corporate culture, where complacency and inertia trumped a sense of urgency. People also better understand the limits of employer paternalism and to what extent a succession of political leaders have failed the test of leadership, perhaps with the exception of Prime Minister Koizumi Junichiro (2001–6) and the reincarnated Abe who disappointed in his first spell as prime minister in 2006–7, but has been more resolute since returning to power in 2012.

## *Crash and Consequences*

The 1980s bubble economy was a period of collective hysteria, a wild time of sudden fortunes, grandiose projects, and ostentatious living that abruptly vanished.[1] Easy money pumped up prices of stock and land, but when the Bank of Japan ratcheted up interest rates six times in 1989, the bubble popped with a vengeance. The crash proved devastating for banks, investors, businesses, and employees. In 2009, two decades on, the stock market average and land prices still hovered near the lows of the early 1990s, down two-thirds from 1989. This implosion unleashed a financial tsunami, leaving a swathe of destruction in its wake. As a result, businessmen, policymakers, regulators, and investors reconsidered the norms and verities of Japan, Inc., and belatedly began retooling economic institutions, practices, and patterns in order to revive the economy.[2] Critics argued that these were largely half-measures that did not go far enough, while others saw betrayal in neoliberal reforms that accentuated disparities between "winners" and "losers."[3]

Shunning layoffs, companies largely kept faith with their regular workers, offering some early retirement, slashing overtime, reducing bonuses (that can amount to 4–6 months' salary), and shifting toward merit pay. The 1990s was a period when the baby boom generation (1947–9), some 7 million strong, were moving up the corporate hierarchy and thus becoming more expensive due to the seniority wage system. This came at a time when companies were feeling the pinch and emphasizing cost-cutting measures. In order to subsidize the high wages of core full-time workers, mostly men, Japanese firms increasingly relied on non-regular workers (part-time, temporary, dispatched, contract workers), mostly women, who were paid much less and enjoyed little job security.

This trend toward the precaritization of the labor

force began in the late 1980s but gained momentum from the 1990s as labor protections were weakened and more sectors were opened to non-regular employment.[4] This trend has increased pressure on the shrinking corps of full-time workers, forcing them to work even longer hours. This interferes with family life and makes it difficult for them to help out at home. Non-regular workers are denied the benefits of their full-time colleagues, but also are not subject to the same demands for lengthy hours and the stress of managing projects and workers. *Karoshi*, death from overwork, is a Japanese term that signifies the dark side of a corporate culture that pressures workers into excessive working hours, in some cases logging well over 100 hours of overtime a month for months in a row. Some commit suicide while others collapse from exhaustion, as workers are inhumanely driven beyond their limits due to a work ethos that puts a premium on dedication and self-sacrifice. Reports of *karoshi* surged in the 1990s, not because this was a new phenomenon, but rather because what was once ignored or implicitly tolerated was no longer acceptable. The media played a critical role in drawing attention to this problem and thereby putting pressure on the government and firms to respond. Now, firms can be held legally liable for *karoshi* and required to pay large settlements to survivors. This is just one example of how Japan is slowly reinventing itself. Economic adversity has prompted introspection and a reassessment of how people live and work, how firms are managed, and what constitutes good governance.

## *1995: A Year of Reckoning*

In 1995, the Great Hanshin-Awaji earthquake in Kobe and the gassing of Tokyo commuters by religious cultists had repercussions well beyond the toll of victims. The earthquake highlighted the government's woeful preparations, while the terrorist attacks in Tokyo's subways heightened a sense of insecurity and concerns that the government could not protect its citizens.

The M7.2 earthquake on January 17, 1995 caused 6,200 deaths and an estimated $100 billion in property damage.[5] About one-third of Kobe was partially or completely destroyed and thousands of families were displaced from their ruined homes. The inept response by the municipal and central governments took the nation by surprise. Incredibly, the city had to improvise a disaster plan. Offers of assistance by foreign relief agencies and US military forces stationed in Japan were spurned, while a call to mobilize the SDF waiting in nearby barracks was inexplicably delayed; they could only act if requested to do so owing to regulations aimed at ensuring civilian control of the military, a legacy of WWII. Deplorable rescue and relief efforts left a lasting impression on a nation that had assumed government officials were competent and prepared. In the aftermath, it was clear to everyone that government officials performed abysmally in coping with the consequences of natural disaster, further undermining the already waning credibility of government institutions. It was especially damning that the yakuza opened the first soup kitchens for Kobe survivors and who could forget that the prime minister first learned about the disaster while listening to the news? Inexcusably, strict enforcement of quarantine regulations prevented overseas search and rescue dogs from entering the country and finding survivors buried under collapsed buildings. There are many such stories of senseless enforcement of regulations that impeded rescue and relief efforts, revealing officials more concerned about rules than helping the people they are supposed to serve.

Over one million volunteers poured into Kobe from all over the country. Volunteers' goodwill and enthusiasm stood in stark contrast to the bureaucrats' stodgy response. Small Japanese NPOs (non-profit organizations) and church groups helped coordinate these volunteer efforts and played a crucial role in providing relief for devastated communities. The media highlighted the critical relief role of NPOs, drawing a sharp contrast with government bungling. This generated public support for NPOs, leading the government to pass an NPO law in 1998 aimed at tapping the potential of civil society. Since then, civil society organizations have mushroomed despite shortcomings in the law and counterproductive government policies that leave NPOs short of funds and professional staff. In Kobe, officials were clueless about how to organize volunteers effectively, but subsequently they and NPOs have been integrated into disaster emergency planning. For the rest of the nation it was a wakeup call to improve disaster resilience, enhance cooperation with civil society groups, and better prepare for the various natural disasters – earthquakes, typhoons, tsunami, and volcanic eruptions – that frequently batter the archipelago.

But nobody was prepared for an act of terror in the heart of Tokyo. On March 20, 1995, members of the Aum Shinrikyo (Supreme Truth Sect) released sarin gas in Tokyo subways, killing 12 people and poisoning a further 5,500 commuters. This brazen attack sent shockwaves throughout the nation, sparking anxieties about what might follow. Authorities also came under fire, as it emerged that the cult was under police surveillance before the attack, raising questions about why they were not apprehended prior to Japan's most serious terrorist incident. Yet again, the government had failed to secure the safety of the people and stood accused of a serious dereliction of duty.

Following the arrest of many of Aum's top leaders (the last fugitive was not arrested until 2012), the nation obsessed about the cult and what its existence and harmful actions signaled about a society that seemed to have lost its way.[6] Prosecution of the cult members spanned two decades, with the final conviction in early 2018. Later that year, cult leader Asahara Shoko and key lieutenants were executed, but questions remain.

Frenzied media coverage examined why this tragedy happened and why the cult appealed to ordinary middle-class youth, some of whom were graduates of elite universities. How was Asahara, the nearly blind leader, able to command such devotion that followers would become terrorists at his bidding? There was speculation that joining the cult constituted repudiation of a society beset with excessive pressures to conform and succeed. Perhaps cultists were reacting against the materialism and spiritual void or, as some asserted, they were lured with promises of power and authority. For ambitious and talented youth, Aum offered a fast track that did not exist in the seniority-based hierarchy of Japanese corporations.

Murakami Haruki, the globally popular writer who also has something of a cult following, wrote *Underground* (2000), a powerful reportage that features interviews with victims of the sarin gas attack and members of Aum. By giving voice to the perceptions and experiences of those involved, Murakami offered a thoughtful counter to media sensationalism. It is a sobering story of disillusion with a work-centered life, materialism, isolation, and anomie that lingers in one's mind. He also conveyed the deep disappointment and anger of victims at the slow and inadequate emergency response. In probing the psychology of the cultists, Murakami concludes that they were fairly ordinary people, not lunatics or villains, an unsettling assessment for those eager to dismiss them as unhinged extremists. The sense of security often taken for granted in Japan was shattered by this assault on society, generating apprehension about what else may be lurking beneath the surface of reassuring appearances. These 1995 events reinforced the post-bubble crisis in confidence at home, a malaise that also influenced global perceptions of Japan.

## Japanization

Columnist William Pesek explains, "It's when entire economies assimilate the worst of Japan's muddle-along ethos and treat the symptoms of their challenges, not the underlying causes. Eventually, years of throwing money at problems that require bold remedies catch up with you: in the form of a funk from which it's near-impossible to escape."[7] Japanization encompasses stagnation, banks on the ropes, zombie companies, overcapacity, and the perils of sustained deflation. The baleful consequences of Japan's bursting bubble were deepened and prolonged by policy drift and half-measures.

Japanization is the policy equivalent of a deer frozen in the headlights. Japan's leaders dithered for a decade, hoping for a brief downturn and quick recovery. Instead, massive bad debt problems festered and too-big-to-fail zombie companies were kept afloat by a steady transfusion of loans they could not repay, compounding the problems. Until the end of the 1990s, the government was complicit with firms' accounting gimmicks that concealed the extent of loan defaults, fearing that spooked markets would plunge into a nosedive. With most major banks overwhelmed by non-performing loans and land values used as collateral evaporating, the government forced rescue mergers between them without addressing the root problems. It also leaned on banks to prop up zombie companies. This temporizing squandered resources and exacerbated deflationary pressures. Zombie firms had incentives to lower prices just to generate enough cash-flow to service interest payments. This deflationary spiral made it difficult for all firms since they also had to lower prices, leaving profits razor-thin or non-existent. So, throwing a lifeline to zombie companies spread the misery and saddled banks with more non-performing loans.

The massive fall in asset prices in the 1990s led healthy companies to repay loans and minimize debt in order to burnish balance sheets and improve credit ratings.[8] When companies do this collectively, demand for loans by creditworthy firms dries up, putting banks in a difficult situation. The Japanese government responded with massive fiscal stimulus packages, but erred in reducing such stimulus too soon. The height of folly came in 1997 when the government decided to raise taxes in order to restore fiscal discipline. This body-slam of austerity stifled a fragile recovery and left banks in worse shape than ever. Following the tax hike debacle, the government tried more fiscal stimulus, but an incipient recovery was nipped in the bud in 2001 when the government raised interest rates and tightened fiscal policy. Despite such counterproductive zigzagging in macro-economic policy, the economy rallied on the strength of a booming Chinese economy and lower oil prices. A tepid recovery from 2002 ended in 2008, however, with the global financial crisis and consequent slump in Japan's export markets.

Botched policymaking during the Lost Decades set the stage for the bold actions promised with Abenomics.[9] It was shock therapy for a moribund economy, simultaneously unleashing monetary and fiscal policy aimed at jolting the economy back to life in order to facilitate urgently needed structural reforms.[10] Yet, more favorable conditions have induced unwarranted complacency and stalled productivity-enhancing reforms and the painful restructuring measures needed for a sustained recovery.

## *Taking Stock*

During the Lost Decades, many Japanese have stoically endured tough times. Layoffs and unemployment have been relatively limited, but the misery index can be measured by other means. Many families took on massive mortgages only to see the value of their property plummet below the debts they owed. This negative equity has depressed consumption as families minimize spending. Suicides surged, as did reports of domestic violence and child abuse. Fathers committed suicide so that their families could collect on life insurance policies, while an affluent society grappled with the sight of homeless men living rough. Young women slipped into the sex industry and there was a rise in juvenile delinquency, while the media proclaimed it was an ice age for young college graduates looking for the kind of stable, well-paid jobs their fathers had. Widening disparities confronted an identity rooted in egalitarian ideals, as younger workers, especially women, were shunted to non-regular jobs where wages and job security are low.[11]

The Japanese media has highlighted the human toll of a stagnant economy while exposing malfeasance in government and promoting greater transparency. It is often criticized for being a government lapdog, but it has grown feistier about the shortcomings of politicians and bureaucrats and helped citizens monitor the government. Thus, it has played a crucial role in changing citizens' perceptions toward the powerful, and made them less trusting and deferential. It has also forced the nation to confront its wartime past. Since the 1990s, Japanese have learned much more about the depredations inflicted by the nation's military across Asia during the 1930s and 1940s, and the media has propelled and shaped this education. On issues ranging from food safety and information disclosure, corruption and privacy protection, the media has held the government accountable. The *kisha* (press) club system, based on privileged access to official sources, promotes self-censorship, but even so the media is fitfully less beholden. Thanks to media coverage, the issues of *kakusa shakai* (income disparities), domestic violence, child abuse, suicide, working poor, mobster influence, systemic corruption, human trafficking, *karoshi*, and many other previously taboo topics are now openly discussed. These problems are not new, but what was largely ignored before the Lost Decades is now the subject of public debate, policy initiatives, legal reforms, and some accountability.[12]

These social ills have become matters of state concern and intervention and the media deserves kudos for pushing that agenda. It is thus a matter for concern that under Prime Minister Abe, press freedom has suffered the hardball tactics of threats, organized campaigns of intimidation, and pressure on advertisers and editors that make journalists more wary about crossing those in power.[13]

## Good Governance

During the 1990s, people confronted the lapses of the elite and the fundamental flaws of a system that has stumbled in meeting the challenges facing the nation. Given the questionable conduct by the men charged with running government, it is not surprising that so many citizens came to support information disclosure legislation. Knowing a little about official shenanigans underscored how important it is to more closely monitor the government. Citizen support for transparency gained momentum in the 1990s, as by 1997 every prefecture and major town passed freedom of information legislation. Spurred by this grassroots rebellion against opaque government, and a series of scandals involving misuse of taxpayer money, the national government also passed information disclosure legislation in 1999 that was implemented in 2001.[14]

The law now facilitates greater disclosure, but government officials controlling the information do not readily comply with the spirit of transparency. Although promoting transparency is still a work in progress, the government is divulging much more about the way it governs and officials now know that their decisions are far more open to scrutiny than ever before. The principle of transparency has been established, but closing loopholes and boosting compliance are an ongoing process because the bureaucracy sees controlling access to information and documents as the basis of its powers and ability to manage debate.

Under Prime Minister Abe there has been some serious backsliding. In 2013, for example, the government passed Special State Secrets legislation that restricts access to documents at the sole discretion of government officials for up to 60 years. There are stiffer penalties for leaking such information, no independent oversight body to review classifications, and no whistleblower protections for disclosure deemed in the public interest. Despite this reversal, a series of scandals related to cronyism and cover-ups implicating Abe led to a sudden sharp plunge in his popularity in the summer of 2017. The one common thread in these cases is the government's mishandling of relevant records. The strong public backlash fed on suspicions that the destruction, alteration or non-disclosure of pertinent documents undermined the principles of transparency and accountability. These principles have taken root and are now viewed as the basis for good governance, a positive element of the third transformation.

### Immigration

The 1990s was a time of experimentation on immigration policy. The government came to regret the 1990 decision to grant *nikkeijin* (Brazilians and other South Americans of Japanese ancestry) open-ended work visas. Samba and samurai cultures proved an awkward fit, especially in the provincial towns where the *nikkeijin* found factory jobs.[15] Contrary to government assumptions, the descendants' DNA did not endow them with necessary language or cross-cultural skills and the government did almost nothing to help them make the transition. When many *nikkeijin* lost their manufacturing jobs in 2008 following the collapse of Lehman Brothers (the subprime mortgage debacle), the government offered "sayonara" airfares to families so they could repatriate, stipulating initially that they could never return. Following public outcry, this condition was ditched in favor of a three-year waiting period. At that time, there were about 320,000 *nikkeijin* living in Japan, dropping to 175,000 by 2016.

The largest minority in Japan is the Chinese community of 650,000, most of whom arrived in the Lost Decades even as bilateral relations soured over unresolved historical grievances. While Chinese migrants have had their share of problems, they have assimilated more easily than Brazilians, especially in terms of language learning due to familiarity with *kanji*. After graduating from Japanese universities, many stay on and work at Japanese firms and some leave to establish their own businesses that leverage their transnational networks.

Ethnic Korean residents (*zainichi*), a population of nearly 600,000, have been here longest. They mostly arrived in the 1930s and 1940s during the wartime, in many cases under duress, and stayed after Japan's defeat. Their status as special permanent residents, even for those who have lived here multiple generations, speaks volumes about the prejudice they encounter. *Zainichi* are in many respects culturally assimilated but continue to be economically and socially marginalized even after a few generations.[16] The Zaitokukai, a rightwing extremist organization with a few thousand members, has been at the forefront of xenophobic anti-*zainichi* agitation since it was founded in 2006. Zaitokukai's Korean-phobic campaign asserts that *zainichi* enjoy advantageous legal rights and are welfare frauds and tax cheats. Zaitokukai conducted several small anti-*zainichi* demonstrations in areas where there are concentrations of ethnic Korean shops and residents, targeting *zainichi* schools with hate speech spewed from megaphones. In response, courts have issued injunctions and imposed fines, while larger counter-demonstrations repudiated the hate-mongering. In 2016 the government enacted a hate speech law aimed at curtailing such discriminatory actions, but this act imposes no penalty for violations.

There are still frequent reports of abuses involving trafficked foreign workers. Following the highly critical 2004 US Trafficking in Persons Report, the Japanese government cracked down on the number of entertainer visas issued to Filipinas who were mostly working in hostess clubs (bars catering to men) by abruptly reducing the total from 80,000 to a few thousand and instituting criteria aimed at making it harder for women to qualify for the visas. But, these good intentions actually made the migrant women workers more vulnerable to abuses by forcing them underground or into paper marriages that makes monitoring of their treatment more difficult and leaves them prey to middlemen in the trafficking business.

## Precaritization and Inequality

During the Lost Decades, *kakusa shakai* (literally: disparity society) thrust its way into public discourse. It wasn't a new phenomenon, but now it is no longer ignored.[17] During the post-WWII era, social cohesion was maintained by a collective belief in everyone sharing the same fate and enjoying similar lifestyles. This myth was sustained in annual government surveys in which most Japanese identified themselves as middle-class. The government and media helped orchestrate this comforting sense of belonging and overstated the egalitarian outcomes of the economic miracle in ways that bestowed legitimacy on the Japan, Inc. model. Thus, when speaking of what was lost in the Lost Decades, loss of faith in that system looms large. The power of the egalitarian myth ensured that inequality remained off the mainstream radar until the twenty-first century because it was a social taboo and the government did not release relevant reports until the DPJ did so in 2009. By 2000, the relative poverty rate, defined as less than one half the median household income, exceeded 15 percent, well above the Organization for Economic Cooperation and Development (OECD) average of 10 percent. By 2016 this rose to 16.3 percent while the percentage of children raised in relative poverty was nearly 14 percent, about 3.5 million children, one of the highest levels in the OECD; only 200,000 of them receive state support. As awareness of such disparities spread, many Japanese came to feel a sense of betrayal.

Neoliberal reforms accentuated differences by accelerating the precaritization of the workforce, but there were other factors at work too. One of these developments is the aging of Japan's population. This has played a role in the widening income gap as the effects of individual human capital investment grow more pronounced over time; university and high school graduate salaries start at similar levels, but widen considerably throughout a career. As the baby boom generation moved up through the corporate hierarchy, this trend has been amplified.

A more important factor in the growing divide, however, is large wage differentials between regular full-time workers and non-regular workers (including contingent workers such as part-time, dispatched, contract, and temporary workers) and the swelling ranks of the latter since the 1980s.[18] As of 2017, non-regular workers account for 38 percent of the workforce, up from 20 percent in 1992. Increasingly, firms are replacing full-time employees with non-regular workers. While the proliferation of less secure, lower paid work boosted profits for Japan, Inc., it has been disastrous for the precariat (>20 million), half of whom are in the ranks of the working poor (>10 million), earning less than ¥2 million a year. These non-regulars earn about 50–60 percent of regular employee wages, and mobility from the precariat to better paid, secure, full-time jobs has been relatively low, especially for those without university degrees, older than 30 years of age and women workers.

Back in the halcyon days of the 1960s economic miracle, there was a shared assumption that what was good for Japan, Inc. was good for Japan. In the 2000s, it emerged that what was good for Japan, Inc. was not good for workers. The transition from the lifetime employment model of secure jobs to one featuring greater risk represents a slow-motion paradigm shift, one driven by a structural shift in the economy from manufacturing to services and facilitated by labor market deregulation since 1999. Regarding these neoliberal reforms, Prime Minister Koizumi Junichiro (2001–6) proclaimed this an era of *jiko sekinen* (self responsibility), meaning that when you are in trouble you are on your own. Incremental labor market deregulation set the stage for the 2008 financial crisis, when 250,000 contract workers in manufacturing were suddenly fired and evicted from company housing, with many literally ending up on the street as they discovered that there was no government safety net for them.

The profound divide in compensation, training, and job security between "haves" (regular workers) and "have nots" (non-regulars) highlights the importance of promoting mobility from second-tier status to the core workforce of regular employment. For most non-regular workers, insecurity and low income are a long-term reality.

This precaritization of the workforce is significant not only because the wage and benefits gap is quite high, but also the productivity of non-regular workers is relatively low because they are not typically given the training that is common for regular workers. So firms save on wages and benefits, but lose out on productivity and worker morale.[19]

There are four main factors that have spurred expansion of the precariat since the late 1980s: greater uncertainty about economic prospects, cost-cutting to keep faith with a core of regular workers in lifetime employment, more married women workers, and the structural shift from manufacturing to services. The discouraging Lost Decades made many firms more anxious about future prospects and cautious about hiring regular workers and the obligations that entails. The low-wage precariat enables firms to preserve the good deal that regular workers have. More married women are now working because their households need additional income; the percentage of dual income households rose from 17 percent in 1980 to nearly two-thirds of married households in 2015. Almost 60 percent of working women are non-regular employees because very few have any other choice, as firms avoid taking on long-term commitments in uncertain times. In addition, many seek flexible working hours to juggle multiple roles as mothers, wives, and caregivers for aging relatives, but even when such responsibilities abate, they remain stuck in non-regular work.

Jobs and family have been pillars of stability in Japan, but both have become less secure. Precaritization is undermining the family by lowering marriage and fertility rates, increasing suicide rates, and contributing to divorce due to the financial distress faced by non-regular households. Only about a third of male non-regular workers in their thirties are married, less than half the marriage rate for regular workers. Given that only 2 percent of babies in Japan are married out of wedlock, the precariat's low marriage rate is contributing to the nation's stark demographic problems that combine a rapidly aging society and a baby drought. Relatively few non-regular workers make the transition to full-time regular work, women much less than men, and this carries major implications for the incidence of poverty. For families where the household head is a non-regular worker, the poverty rate is 41 percent and the poverty exit rate is very low. Social spending on low-income households is also low. Thus, the precariat of non-regular workers trapped in low-paid, dead-end jobs with limited job security and career prospects, is becoming an underclass that challenges Japan's egalitarian values and norms.

This problem gained more media attention after the 2008 global financial crisis. At the outset of 2009, a coalition of NPOs established a tent-village and soup kitchen for the newly unemployed, many of whom had become homeless. These victims of the economic crisis gathered in a central Tokyo park across from the Ministry of Health, Labor, and Welfare, pressuring the government to do something to help. This also shone a withering spotlight on the companies that were firing these workers and the conservative politicians who had sponsored labor market deregulation that reduced worker protections.

The LDP came under fire for enacting various neo-liberal reforms that accentuated disparities and pre-caritization. The public backlash was strong, helping oust the LDP and catapult the DPJ into a landslide victory in the 2009 elections.[20]

The changing employment paradigm, and its

harmful consequences, propelled political change, but this insurrection was short lived as the LDP, led by Abe Shinzo, regained power in 2012 on the strength of the pro-business program known as Abenomics.[21] The disparities and the precariat remain, but the DPJ imploded. This is partly due to its own incompetence, but also, as discussed in chapter 3, because it questioned the pro-US alliance and pro-business consensus that had been the foundation of the Japan, Inc. model. The DPJ also had the misfortune of being in charge during the seismic and nuclear cataclysms of 2011.

## *Natural Disaster: The 2011 Tsunami*

In some respects, the tsunami that slammed Japan on March 11, 2011 marked the end of the Lost Decades, precipitating the LDP's comeback. The subsequent election of Prime Minister Abe, partially propelled by the flawed disaster response and recovery efforts, ended the policy discontinuities and administrative instability of revolving prime ministers (six between 2006 and 2012) as the nation began climbing out of the deep hole it had descended into.

The record M9.0 magnitude earthquake triggered a huge tsunami that devastated coastal communities along a 500 km stretch of Japan's remote northeastern coastline, a region known as Tohoku.[22] In some places, the tsunami crested at 38 meters above sea level, reaching above and beyond the tsunami stones

– placed as a warning to future generations not to build below the line of inundation – that dot a coastal region that has suffered numerous ruinous waves over the centuries, this being the third since the late nineteenth century. But every generation makes its own mistakes even if it is only repeating the past mistakes of others.

The seismic tremors caused relatively little direct damage to buildings or infrastructure, testimony to strict building codes, but were felt as far away as Kyoto. Tokyo towers swayed for several minutes and train services were suspended, stranding commuters, but there was a sigh of relief that nothing big toppled. Up in Tohoku, the numerous tunnels for roads through the hilly coastline remained intact. It is also remarkable, given the apocalyptic scenes, that less than 20,000 people died in the tsunami, a testimony to disaster drills and sustained public campaigns to raise awareness about the need to prepare for the worst and to where people should evacuate. Just a week before the tsunami struck, there had been a school evacuation drill to commemorate the 1933 tsunami. Knowing what to do made a difference, even if some were lulled into a false sense of security in towns nestled behind 8-meter tsunami walls, considered sufficient for any eventuality. It also helped that the tsunami struck during the day when schools were in session and people were awake, facilitating evacuations.

The sheer devastation is impossible to describe.

Entire towns were transformed into masses of rubble, with houses and buildings torn from their foundations. Cars were strewn randomly and boats marooned far inland, while a sea of bare foundations attested to where communities once thrived. The detritus of families was strewn about with photo albums buried in mud alongside stuffed animals while flotsam and jetsam emblazoned the tops of utility poles and fences along 15-meter embankments. Here and there skeletons of buildings stood out from the flattened landscape, some with cars teetering on top, while missing walls opened private interiors to the gaze of outsiders. Peering down from hillside cemeteries where ancestors remained safe, there were vistas of pulverized towns, reduced to mounds of debris, crumpled seawalls and broken rail lines dangling above where embankments had been swept away. Along this saw-tooth coastline there were also communities untouched by the ravages of nature because they faced away from the tsunami, reminders of what the surrounding ruination used to look like.

Unlike in Kobe in 1995, the government responded quickly to the disaster as Prime Minister Kan Naoto (2010–11) mobilized the SDF within hours to conduct search and rescue operations. In much more difficult terrain in a sprawling disaster zone, where access was impeded by blocked roads and damaged airports and harbors, the SDF won kudos for their actions. In Operation Tomodachi (Friendship), US troops were also dispatched to assist their SDF counterparts, quickly clearing Sendai airport to facilitate delivery of relief supplies, touching the hearts of a stunned nation while playing a prominent role in the emergency response. Beginning with search and rescue operations, and continuing with immediate relief and longer-term support services, civil society organizations played a key role in disaster response efforts. Neighborhood associations provided organization and solidarity as locals relied as much as possible on their own resources and ingenuity. They got major support from domestic and international NGOs that rapidly deployed their staff to make assessments, and then mobilized resources and networks to raise money, appeal for volunteers, organize them, and provide assistance to shattered communities. Using social media, it was possible for relatives and friends that had lost contact due to the calamity to reconnect. NGOs also relied on social media to assess needs, manage the influx of supplies and volunteers, and distribute what was needed to where it was required. In contrast to Kobe, where volunteers streamed into the city only to find that their enthusiasm and compassion were squandered due to a lack of institutional support, volunteers in Tohoku had a greater impact even if the numbers were lower, precisely because local institutions and civil society groups managed the influx.

Recovery is still an ongoing and uneven process. Despite some inspiring stories of recovery, for many towns and their residents the future looks bleak as 3.11 has hastened ongoing decline. Certainly, there are some impressive examples of progress, but stagnation is returning as the government reduces massive construction budgets that had pumped up the local economy. It is hard to be optimistic about prospects for this region because the exodus of youth accelerated after the tsunami, leaving behind less resilient, older communities. And, with the Tokyo Olympics looming, and massive construction projects underway, Tohoku is again facing marginalization as its needs are slipping down the list of national priorities.

## Nuclear Disaster

The three nuclear reactor meltdowns at the Fukushima Daichi plant in March 2011 magnified public anxieties exponentially, well beyond the battered tsunami zone, making this a national and international disaster.[23] The powerful quake and 15-meter tsunami that inundated the Fukushima Daiichi nuclear plant were the proximate causes that led to the loss of electricity and the failure of backup generators at the plant. The ensuing cessation of the cooling systems caused three meltdowns within the first 80 hours. It appears that the earthquake toppled electricity pylons while onsite backup generators did not work and batteries soon ran out of power, causing a station blackout. Plant staff improvised, even hooking up car batteries, but to no avail. It was a chaotic situation, with plant workers trying to read emergency manuals by flashlight while getting contradictory and confusing instructions from their superiors. Within days of the meltdowns, three hydrogen explosions ripped apart reactor containment buildings, spewing radiation into the skies while gusty spring winds blew the toxic clouds far afield.

There were no fatalities in the accident, but the lives of over 150,000 nuclear evacuees were turned upside down and their communities decimated. Six years on, there were still some 100,000 nuclear refugees who could not return to their homes, as a pared down exclusion zone remained in force and nobody wanted to return to the ghost towns in surrounding areas. Some workers at the plant suffered extremely high doses of radiation and a number of elderly patients died as a result of being evacuated, but not from radiation. Studies continue on the incidence of thyroid cancer among children.

Investigations into the accident have established that the crisis response was inadequate because there was a lack of emergency procedures, poor communication within the government and between officials and TEPCO (Tokyo Electric Power Company, the utility company that operated the Fukushima power plant). Moreover, politicians lacked knowledge about nuclear issues and crisis management, and did not get sufficient support or information from the utility or bureaucrats to cope with the crisis.

For quite some time after the accident, TEPCO tried to blame Prime Minister Kan for delaying and mismanaging its crisis response, but the accusations were groundless. Outside of the nuclear village of advocates, Kan was the hero of the moment and the public lauded him for idling all of the nation's reactors for extensive safety checks and passing legislation to promote renewable energy. Until October 2012, when it finally admitted responsibility for the disaster, TEPCO claimed disingenuously that it was a Black Swan event and thus it was blameless.

A week before the 3.11 tsunami, the Nuclear Industrial Safety Agency (NISA) had approved TEPCO's application to extend the operating life of its 40-year-old reactor at Fukushima, but issued a warning about stress cracks in the backup generators that left them vulnerable to inundation that would leave them unable to function. NISA said they should be replaced and advised that they be relocated since they were sited on the ocean side of the plant and below it, thus at high risk of flooding in the event of a tsunami. In the event, the backup generators were submerged and conked out.

TEPCO defended itself by asserting that the 15-meter tsunami that swamped the plant and caused the station blackout was *sotegai* (inconceivable), but it turns out that TEPCO conducted in-house simulations in 2009 that suggested the possibility of a 15-meter tsunami. Not only was TEPCO aware that there was a risk of a monster wave, it also considered building a bigger sea wall to protect the plant from the risk it knew existed. In the end, however, TEPCO decided not to build the $1 billion sea wall that would probably have prevented the meltdowns, what would have been a bargain in retrospect given the estimated $626 billion taxpayers will pay over the next four decades for decontamination and decommissioning the stricken reactors.

## *Nuclear Renaissance?*

The nuclear village is eager to restart idled reactors because they are more profitable to operate and represent massive investments and debts that need to be repaid. The utilities argue that it is cheaper than importing fuel for thermal power plants, but the price of power is in the eye of the beholder. In the view of the Japanese public, the real cost of nuclear power is apparent in the devastated lives of Fukushima residents forced to evacuate their ancestral homes, in the anxieties about children's radiation exposure, in the loss of livelihoods for farmers and fishermen, in addition to the costs of decontamination, disposal of radioactive waste and fuel rods from the stricken reactors, decommissioning, compensation for the displaced, and the massive government bailout of TEPCO. For the vast majority of the Japanese public, the longstanding mantra about nuclear power being safe, cheap, and reliable is a joke in poor taste.

In 2014, Abe reinstated nuclear energy into the national energy strategy with a target of generating 20–22 percent of Japan's electricity capacity by 2030. This would require restarting 30 reactors in total. Restarts are dependent on the decision of NISA's successor, the Nuclear Regulatory Authority (NRA) that introduced stricter regulations and required utilities to upgrade safety systems. The NRA is subject to countervailing political pressures; the central government and reactor hosting communities that favor restarts, and most of the public that opposes doing so based on safety concerns. Hosting communities are mostly in favor of restarts because idled reactors do not generate subsidies and revenues that constitute the main source of town budgets. These towns were chosen to host reactors because they were remote and suffering from economic decline and depopulation, so they are dependent on the nuclear lifeline. Neighboring towns are not so keen because they assume all the same risks without the benefits and now, under the 30 km expanded evacuation zone instituted by the NRA, they are responsible for developing evacuation plans and conducting drills without sufficient resources to do so.

The lessons of Fukushima are in many respects being ignored. The NRA mandated safety upgrades of facilities, but has made less progress on the software of safety that contributed to the debacle: worker training, crisis management, and planning for worst-case scenarios. Fukushima demonstrated the folly of wishing risk away, but the NRA and utilities appear more eager to hasten restarts than to take the time necessary to manage risk more effectively. Moreover, there have been significant advances in seismic science regarding fault lines since the reactor sites were selected back in the 1970s. What was deemed safe then may no longer be so. This issue is crucial in a nation that experiences more magnitude 6+ earthquakes than any other nation where reactors are operated. New assessments suggest some reactors the utilities have restarted, or want to bring online, are located close to active fault lines and others are endangered by volcanic eruptions.

By 2018, utilities had NRA permission to restart 14 reactors. Courts have issued injunctions barring some restarts, as judges have sided with citizens in voicing skepticism about the utilities' upgraded safety reassurances, disaster countermeasures, evacuation plans, and dangerous siting. The utilities generally appeal and prevail, but a groundswell of opposition to reactor restarts has slowed the nuclear revival that Prime Minister Abe promised when campaigning in 2012. He represents the vested interests of the nuclear village of pro-nuclear advocates and has worked hard to help the industry overcome a perfect storm of safety lapses, strong public opposition, and ballooning costs for the Fukushima cleanup.

Given the high costs of nuclear energy, the absence of a permanent site to store radioactive waste, and the potential risks of another Fukushima, the public favors phasing it out as soon as possible. Meanwhile, the feed-in tariff introduced in 2012 by Prime Minister Kan had within five years boosted renewable energy capacity, mostly solar, by the equivalent of 13 nuclear reactors at a fraction of the cost and time required to build one reactor.

### *Game Changer?*

The shock of 3.11, and the scale of devastation, generated national solidarity, an outpouring of donations, an
influx of volunteers, and displayed the stoic dignity of
the survivors. But Tohoku became hostage to politics,
and the unwavering resolve to rejuvenate the region
soon faded. This grim outcome is not only due to the
failures of politicians, who have a lot to answer for
and could have made more of a difference. There were
high hopes at the time that the natural and nuclear
disasters would jolt the nation out of its torpor and
become a catalyst for sweeping reform, with parties
putting aside their differences and working together
to not only rebuild Tohoku, but also transform Japan.
These hopes were dashed, and in terms of policy
innovations, the crisis was largely wasted.[24]

Yet, the catastrophe did play an important role
in leading to a change of government in 2012. Abe
returned to power by taking advantage of the DPJ's
shortcomings and offering a vision of hope. Abenomics
represented an exit strategy from sagging confidence
and economic stagnation. At the close of 2017, the
Nikkei stock average closed at nearly 23,000, rising
140 percent since Abe took power five years earlier,
but still well below the 39,000 peak in 1989, some
three decades on. Is this just another bubble waiting
to pop?

Although a relapse can't be ruled out, Japan seems
to have rebounded from the doldrums of the Lost

Decades. The lingering sense of decline, however, leaves a majority of Japanese convinced that the nation's best years are behind it. And the gathering problems of an aging and shrinking population are not going away, casting a cloud over the nation's future prospects. These problems are driving the third transformation, but also imperil it precisely because Abe has not used his considerable clout to make much headway on mitigating these challenges. He has also had to contend with a culture of dissent that opposes the neoliberal agenda of the third transformation.

# 5

# Dissent

To understand Japan it is essential to peer behind the façade of harmony and prevailing stereotypes of a conformist citizenry prone to groupthink and inclined to be overly deferential to authority. There is a rich tradition of reifying these traits despite considerable evidence to the contrary. This essentialist approach emphasizes what is singular and exotic about a modern nation, where young Japanese seem to be less beholden to traditional norms and establishing new ones. In Japan there is a veritable cottage industry of local writers whose goal is to explain to the Japanese who they are and why their culture, traditions, thinking, language, aesthetics, agricultural techniques, and way of life is superior and unique. This *nihonjinron* school of thought taps into an apparently endless appetite for such self-congratulatory assessments, although the heyday was in the 1980s, a time when Japan seemed ascendant and invincible. The emphasis on maintaining a façade of harmony is one of many mechanisms for stifling and marginalizing dissent and sustaining the myth there is none. There is a lot of dissent in Japan, but it is discouraged and suppressed at many levels, including by the state, employers, and even neighborhood associations. And, because the cost of dissent can be high, it is often subtle and goes undetected.

The monolithic images that emerge are based on what can actually be observed in society but marginalize aspects that do not fit the narrative. So, it is true that Japanese are often deferential, uncomfortable with confrontation, eager to smooth things over, inclined to be part of a group, and subsume their individuality to nurture solidarity. Harmony, *wa*, is desirable, and much will be sacrificed to maintain it, but this is only part of the story.

Before 1945, enforcement mechanisms against dissent were very powerful, and included reduced rations, police intimidation, imprisonment, and torture. Since 1945 these enforcement mechanisms abruptly weakened, especially for visible dissent. Yet there is a rich tradition of dissent in Japan – political and artistic – that subverts notions of a society that eschews open disagreements and embraces Confucian codes of hierarchy. Overall, people tend to be passive about politics, disinclined to activism, and don't want to be the protruding nail because they have been told since they were children that it will get hammered down. Risk aversion is inculcated in children and the lessons of not edging out on a limb are carried forward through careful and prudent choices in education, jobs, marriage, investments, and expressing opinions. The stigma of public shaming or ostracism is a powerful deterrent. Notions of a monolithic national character, however, do not capture much

observable reality and promote the notion that DNA
or culture is destiny. Spend much time in Japan, and
you will encounter warm, friendly, and spontaneous
people who are not programmed automatons and do
not exactly exude many of the traits discussed above,
although they can. More recently, some of the postwar enforcement mechanisms have broken down too,
but new ones have emerged such as the Special State
Secrets Law (2013) and conspiracy legislation (2017)
championed by the Abe government. Overall, however, Japan has become a more diverse and tolerant
society in ways that allow people to openly embrace
an expanding range of diverse lifestyles at odds with
mainstream norms. The tricky part of breaking down
stereotypes is that they are not entirely wrong, but they
are seriously misleading if projected monolithically,
which is the crux of these sweeping generalizations.

## *The Nobility of Failure*

Dissent is thus tricky terrain in a society where it is
often denigrated, suppressed, or kept out of sight. The
manufacturing of harmony and consensus is backed
by the powers of Japan, Inc.[1] The odds are not in favor
of those who stand up to these powers, if only because
they are institutionalized, command the resources of
the state and business establishment, and focus on
pursuing clear goals that involve not conceding. As
such, they have enormous advantages over activists
and dissidents who are mostly amateurs with limited

resources at their disposal. These inspired volunteers draw power from their principles and from the abuses and misdeeds they seek to redress, but confront those who get paid to stifle and ignore their voices. There is a degree of vindication in showing defiance, express-ing dissent, throwing off the weight of conformity, gaining small concessions, delaying the inevitable, raising public awareness, and exposing abuses. Ivan Morris has dubbed Japan's admiration for such lost causes the "nobility of failure."[2] Japan's history is full of inspiring characters that put their lives on the line, knowing they will lose, but find redemption of sorts by establishing the purity of their motives and their willingness to sacrifice. In fact, there is a longstand-ing tradition of respecting dissent and dissent being effective.

Ironically, in supposedly conformist, stable Japan, one is spoiled for choice in selecting examples of dis-sent. Some involve strikes and mass protests, some include citizens pursuing their cause in the courts, while others involve campaigns of civil disobedi-ence. What is striking is just how much dissent is manifested in a nation where harmony is the alleged default mode. This aspect of Japan is often over-looked, probably because Japanese are often stoic and persevere uncomplainingly in the face of grim and unacceptable situations, and manage crisis with a surprising degree of equanimity. As an outsider living in Japan since 1987, I often wondered why people were not angrier given they have so much to be fed up with. Rather than apathy, this getting on with life approach expresses a *shoganai* (it can't be helped) sense of resignation in the face of circumstances that appear impervious to change or reform. But sometimes, among some people, tolerance of the intolerable is suspended and the accumulated grievances and sense of injustice explodes when some imperceptible line is crossed … and then abruptly recedes again in a collective forgetting, simmering as time passes, and a rosier nostalgia emerges from the painful and disharmonious memories.

In 1945 the Americans got things off to a good start by releasing all political prisoners from Japan's jails, including leftists and others who had stood up against the repressive forces of militarism that enveloped wartime Japan. The wartime dissidents were assumed to be on the same side and share similar values as those who wanted to reform Japan, an assessment SCAP came to quickly reconsider. The US also wrote a range of civil liberties into the new 1947 Constitution. Japanese became citizens, no longer subjects of the Emperor (who renounced his divinity in 1946), and they had the right to assembly and freedom of expression. But the Americans also taught the Japanese state how to suppress dissent in more sophisticated ways than in the past. They did not tolerate untethered freedom of expression, as there were taboo topics that the media was not allowed to discuss, for example the atomic bombings, crimes committed by US troops, or the establishment of brothels for them by the Japanese government.[3] American censorship was extensive and also produced a desired level of self-censorship as the Japanese media adjusted, drawing on wartime experiences. The media also could not report about the "apartheid" metro system in occupied Japan, wherein certain train cars would have a white line painted on them, signifying they were reserved for occupation forces and Japanese were not allowed. Film director Ozu Yasujiro managed to sneak a few fleeting shots of these white-striped train carriages past the censors in *Late Spring* (1949), and along with Akira Kurosawa engaged in as much artful subversion as possible. Overall, censorship was a godsend for authorities – SCAP and Japanese – in dealing with dissent by muzzling it. So, the democratic revolution from above was selective and incomplete. Lessons were learned. The media could "unhappen" events by ignoring them, a situation we discuss below regarding anti-nuclear demonstrations.

SCAP legalized unions and the right to collective bargaining. Union membership exploded because organizers effectively tapped into workers' discontent about low pay and miserable working and living conditions. Unions were aggressive, sometimes engaging in lockouts of management and taking over the factories. Rampant inflation and shortages of food and other daily necessities added fuel to the fires of unrest. These grievances sparked radical action by unions, drawing the attention of the Americans. Moreover, Japanese politicians and corporate leaders lobbied

SCAP, playing on American fears about a red menace and the prospects of a delayed economic recovery.

On February 1, 1947, MacArthur banned a general strike, signaling an end to SCAP tolerance and emboldening management. Unionists were shocked that MacArthur had betrayed them, abandoning strong support for the labor movement as one of many initiatives aimed at democratizing Japan and countering the excessive concentration of power in the pre-war era that enabled the militarists to embark on their rampage in Asia. This so-called "reverse course" marked a watershed in the occupation as the Cold War escalated and the emphasis shifted toward ensuring Japan became a showcase for the advantages of the US capitalist system.[4] In the space of two short years, the Americans ditched initially punitive policies and efforts to reinvent Japan in favor of making Japan into an economic success story. That meant working with the conservative political and corporate elite that had supported the war effort. But there were new enemies to vanquish and new priorities as rivalry with the Soviet Union intensified dramatically in Europe and Asia. From a communist insurgency in Greece to the civil war in China between the Kuomintang backed by the US and Mao Zedong's communist forces, Washington saw the hand of Moscow. In this situation, tolerance for leftists and communists vanished as SCAP launched a red purge aimed at rooting them out of the unions, media, politics, and elsewhere.

From 1947, Japanese companies engaged in

union-busting tactics, using thugs to intimidate and attack organizers, and pressuring workers to give up their union membership in favor of in-house, company-sponsored unions. Those that refused got fired. This taming of the labor movement was carried out by Japan, Inc., sometimes in cahoots with the yakuza, demonstrating how the Establishment episodically relied on the underworld to do its dirty work. By the time the Occupation ended in 1952, the confrontational union movement had not yet been obliterated, but momentum was on the side of management as it established tame unions to nurture the cooperative industrial relations that suited Japan, Inc.

Time was running out for Japan's coalmines in the 1950s as the national energy strategy was shifting toward oil. In Kyushu, miners at the Miike mine balked at management's plans to downsize the workforce. Mitsui was eager to cut losses and wanted to crush the local miners' union by firing some 1,000 workers identified as troublemakers, targeting union activists and members of leftist political parties. The situation came to a head in 1960, overlapping the massive demonstrations against the revision and extension of the US–Japan Treaty of Mutual Security, known as Anpo, discussed below, that eventually brought down Prime Minister Kishi Nobusuke. Sōhyō, at the time Japan's largest trade union federation, provided financial support to the strikers during the ensuing 312-day strike. During this ten-month acrimonious confrontation, Mitsui hired thugs to intimidate and beat strikers, sparking violent clashes. In the end, Mitsui had its way, prevailing against the union dissenters.

These are the dark origins of Japan's famously harmonious industrial relations. This apparent harmony is seen as an exemplar of the benefits of cooperative ties between managers and employees, but in the first 15 years after 1945, such labor clashes and union busting were common. At the same time that the brass knuckles came out, the status quo rhetoric about harmony got pumped up too because it incited people to police each other and themselves; it was a cross-class version of "soft power." The vast improvement in living and working conditions from the mid-1950s onward, however, eased workplace tensions and worker grievances. Moreover, labor unions had a political voice in the Socialist Party, a powerful opposition party that was winning over one third of the popular vote and confronting the LDP in the Diet. It also helped that rapid growth did not bring gross income disparities due to relatively egalitarian wage policies.

## *Anpo 1960*

The political battle lines were clear between the central government and hundreds of thousands of demonstrators who took to the streets of Tokyo and elsewhere in Japan from 1959 to protest security ties with the US and the threat of nuclear war.[5] In 1960, the broader public became aroused by the pending renewal and revision of the Treaty of Mutual Cooperation and Security with the US, known by its Japanese acronym Anpo. This term is also widely used to refer to the anti-treaty movement that involved a broad cross-section of Japanese society protesting the alliance and the high-handed tactics of Prime Minister Kishi. The US had arrested him as a Class A war crimes suspect due to his role in the wartime Tojo Hideki cabinet, but he was never prosecuted. In one of the more incredible, if not dispiriting, comeback stories, Kishi became prime minister only a dozen years after the war ended and less than a decade after his release from Sugamo prison where he had been incarcerated for over three years. The street protests were thus opposed to an alliance that offended pacifist sentiments and a prime minister who was part of the cabal of militarists who lead Japan into a catastrophic war, devastating the homeland, and wreaking havoc in much of Asia.

The 1951 security treaty had been negotiated while Japan was still under US occupation and was ratified by the Diet without full knowledge of the provisions. Moreover, there was no input from the free press or elected representatives of a vibrant democracy the Americans were proudly nurturing. The occupation ended in 1952, but for many Japanese, the continued presence of large numbers of American troops scattered on bases across the archipelago, and the lingering US control of Okinawa, suggested an ongoing occupation. So, when the government announced plans to renew Anpo, this was the first chance for many dissenting Japanese to voice their opposition by taking to the streets, with rallies peaking in May and June 1960. At the height of the protests, organizers estimated 330,000 demonstrators from all walks of life surrounded the Diet building. Nearly everyone was peaceful, but the more extreme tactics of the leftist Zengakuren (All Japan League of Student Self-Governments) drew considerable public criticism, as did rightwing goons and police counterattacks; the public condemned violence on both sides. Some of the protests were creative and made the case that dissent was compatible with Japanese culture and history; the long undulating snake dances of protestors in front of the Diet in central Tokyo evoked traditional Japanese *matsuri* (festivals), a carnival atmosphere amidst political confrontation.[6]

There were in fact some revisions in the treaty that the public might have welcomed if the mood had not become so polarized due to Kishi's strong-arm tactics, ramming the legislation through the Diet in the absence of the Japan Socialist Party (JSP), the main opposition. The JSP had been engaged in a sit-in to disrupt Diet proceedings, but Kishi had them forcibly removed, and then renewed the revised security treaty. He was deeply resented for an authoritarian style involving such critical legislation in ways that subverted democracy. Kishi came to power in a backroom deal and was an unappreciated reminder of how the wartime elite had burrowed back into

power under American auspices. He was leader of the
Liberal Democratic Party (LDP) that was established
in 1955 as a merger of the two main conservative
parties in order to strengthen support for the security alliance. The merger, arranged and funded by the
CIA, launched a party that has served as the voice of
Washington in Japan ever since.

In this context, there was not much public appreciation for treaty revisions that, for example, banned
the US military from intervening inside Japan and
also required consultations between the governments
regarding overseas deployments of US troops. Even
with those changes, it remained an unequal relationship in Washington's favor and one-sided because
Tokyo's pacifist constitution meant Japan's military
forces could not come to the aid of US military forces,
even if the latter were defending Japan when they
came under attack. Many Japanese worried that the
alliance would not make them safer and in fact make
Japan a target. Indeed, in May 1960 the Soviet Union
made just such a threat against unspecified nations
that allowed the US to launch spy planes as Japan regularly did.

Dissent in 1960 was partially successful. The security treaty was passed despite the protests, but Kishi
was forced to step down. And, a planned visit by US
President Dwight Eisenhower was called off due to
concerns about ensuring his safety. Public defiance
by a broad cross-section of society reflected frustra-
tion with party politics and anger that the pacifist

principles of the Constitution were being betrayed.
Japan had come a long way in the two decades since
launching a war at Pearl Harbor in 1941. The public
protested militarism, the security alliance, return of
wartime leaders to power, and the cupidity of mainstream politics, exuberantly exercising new democratic freedoms unimaginable during the war. Anpo
sowed the seeds of grassroots activism in Japan,
inspiring a new generation and highlighting opportunities that led to a flowering of civic movements.[7]

## Beiheiren

From the mid-1960s, students and intellectuals took
up where Anpo left off, challenging the entrenched
Establishment. Anpo quickly faded, but it was crucial to the subsequent student movement as a model
for the theater of politics and by creating a space for
dissent. Protestors had rewritten the script in the
security treaty drama by toppling Kishi even if the
ending remained unchanged. An energized public
was exercising their democratic rights and taking on
the powerful forces of the state and the unpopular
alliance with the US.

In 1965, prominent intellectuals established
Beiheiren (Peace in Vietnam Committee) to protest
the Vietnam War and Japan's complicity, by virtue
of war-related procurements, including napalm, that
amounted to $1 billion a year between 1966 and 1971.
Scarcely 20 years after Japan's war ended in Asia, the

ideologically charged American intervention touched a raw nerve among Japan's pacifists, especially because it was harming fellow Asians. Pan-Asianism had been invoked to justify Japan's wartime invasions across the region under the banner of colonial liberation and now lingered as a basis for solidarity. Beiheiren was never a mass organization but was prominent in public discourse and tapped into anti-war sentiments; polls in 1965 indicated 75 percent of Japanese opposed the US bombing of North Vietnam. Beiheiren's criticism of the Vietnam War and the US resonated with the public and played a role in sparking the student movement that spread over campuses and spilled into the streets. Between 1964 and 1973, Japanese perceptions of the US soured dramatically, and it seems the Vietnam War was a major factor, as it went from the most favored nation of 49 percent to one that only 18 percent admired. Beiheiren's influence was amplified by a media-savvy presence, including outreach to overseas intellectuals and support for the American peace movement. Curiously, it was not monolithic ideologically as prominent leftists including Nobel laureate Oe Kenzaburo and Oda Makoto joined forces with rightwing writers like Ishihara Shintaro who subsequently became a famous firebrand politician. It sponsored visits to Japan by luminaries such as Jean-Paul Sartre, Simone de Beauvoir, and Howard Zinn, and helped spark a movement that drew considerable support from ordinary citizens.

## Student Movement

Drawing on the energy and experience of Anpo and the dissenting stance of Beiheiren, from 1967 the student movement on university campuses escalated into major clashes, with police and educators, but also between leftist radical groups. Zengakuren was well established on many campuses and was at the vanguard of the student movement and protests that targeted the arrival at Sasebo naval base of the USS Enterprise, a nuclear-powered aircraft carrier, deployed for the Vietnam War. The visit drew extensive media coverage because it coincided with Japan's growing anti-war movement. This was not the first nuclear-powered US naval vessel in Japan – others had transited – but this symbol of American military might, targeting the Vietnamese, was suspected of violating the third of the Three Non-Nuclear Principles of Prime Minister Sato (1965–71) (see chapter 3). Washington was adamant about not declaring whether its vessels were carrying nuclear weapons, and Tokyo refrained from pressing for clarification, the alliance equivalent of "don't ask, don't tell." At Sasebo there were pitched battles between student protestors armed with wooden staves confronted by heavily armed riot police who beat and gassed them. The Enterprise docked, but the various student groups were not about to concede and throughout the year at various places violent clashes escalated in tandem with the Vietnam War. Overall the anti-war movement was non-violent, but radical groups stole the limelight with their aggressive tactics and rioting, closing down shopping districts, disrupting transport, and provoking the police. Student groups occupied university administration buildings and confronted unsupportive faculty, forcing the suspension of classes at dozens of elite Japanese institutions. Now students had more time on their hands and were released from the pressures of exams. They could also rally against the poor level of university education in cramped, aged facilities, with overcrowded classes and professors going through the motions. High school students would have to go through an initiation ritual, so-called "examination hell," meaning endless hours of studying for university entrance exams that emphasize rote memorization. The lucky entrants then confronted the demoralizing reality of a dysfunctional university system. So, there was much to protest about in addition to the war.[8]

Another issue was the disposition of Okinawa. The US-controlled "Cold War" islands host most of the US forces based in Japan, facilitating the projection of American military power.[9] On April 28, 1969, the anniversary of Japan's "abandonment" of Okinawa to American military administration in exchange for ending the occupation and regaining national sovereignty, there were nationwide protests in favor of reversion to full Japanese sovereignty. In Tokyo, Zengakuren and other radical groups, including workers, taunted police, erected barricades, and instigated violent street battles. Prime Minister Sato had just negotiated the forthcoming return of the islands in 1972, but this "reversion" allowed the US bases to remain.

Despite the zenith of protests and dissent in 1969, not much changed. The conservative LDP held elections and increased its majority, the US alliance remained robust, Washington still used bases in Japan for its war in Vietnam, the capitalist system remained intact, and university education remained woeful. More importantly, public opinion turned on the protestors, largely due to violent incidents, but also because they had inconvenienced commuters and shoppers. The media and state portrayed them as confrontational troublemakers sabotaging social harmony, thus "betraying" national character.

By 1970 the security treaty was renewed, Okinawa was settled and the objective conditions for revolution had deteriorated, as during the 1960s gross national product quadrupled and per capita annual income rose from less than $400 to almost $1,300. Rising living standards and better prospects in an expanding economy took the wind out of the sails of campus radicals. But hardline groups had tasted violence, embraced confrontation, and dreamed of revolution. The experience of 1969 radicalized the New Left and violence was justified as a tool for instigating the revolution, and not just in Japan. The dissenters were hard-core, ideologically motivated youth who saw themselves as the global vanguard and as such inclined to endure and demand sacrifice.

If the 1960s was anti-government and anti-war, the 1970s was a venting of broader frustrations and a lashing out at the status quo. It was also a time when radical groups splintered and turned on each other, often over obscure ideological rifts. These power plays made violence and self-denial the currency of revolutionary zeal. This was very different from the "let's make love not war" peace movement in the US and more along the lines of the Weather Underground[10] or Germany's Red Army Faction; the hardcore vibe valued abstinence, personal austerity, and willingness to sacrifice, and was dismissive of petit bourgeois comforts. This was a time of purges and infighting, self-criticism sessions, accusations of treason, and hyper factionalism. The main internecine combatants were the Kakumara-ha and the Chukaku-ha, who disagreed violently about the best way to achieve the desired revolution and were willing to beat and kill each other for the cause. This bloody infighting turned much of the public against leftists. In public memory, the single most horrific episode was the Asama-Sanso incident in 1972. This incident involved Rengo Sekigun, a merger of two hardcore revolutionary groups that remained divided even after ostensibly joining forces. About two dozen members decamped to a cabin in the mountains of Gunma for training exercises. Differences over tactics and arcane ideological points of view evolved into bitter infighting, leading to trials, torture, and hangings, graphically portrayed in Wakamatsu Koji's epic film *United Red Army* (2011). These purges continued over several weeks in the winter cold, with some of the unfortunate members freezing to death after being banished outside. Dying was dismissed as a sign of insufficient revolutionary zeal.

The police closed in and arrested members when they were out shopping for supplies and others who were trying to escape the camp, leaving five at large who sought refuge in a mountain lodge, Asama Sanso. The police laid siege to the lodge for ten days, while the Rengo Sekigun members held out by throwing bombs and firing gunshots. When the police finally stormed the lodge, two officers were killed and another wounded. Under police questioning, details emerged about the purges that led to the discovery of a grave containing the battered frozen corpses of a dozen Rengo Sekigun members. This entire incident drew extensive television coverage as the nation watched the shocking denouement. But it was the gruesome grave and the horrific story of the purge that seared a place in the collective memory where nightmares are stored. From radical underdogs taking on the state and earning public sympathy, they became reviled crackpots whose barbaric orgy of bloodletting sparked an overwhelming and lasting backlash.

## Narita International Airport

Narita is one of Tokyo's two airports and a site of prolonged contestation between the state and citizens,
this time involving an unlikely alliance of farmers and
young leftists. The project was conceived in the late
1960s when Japan was growing apace and it seemed
that Tokyo needed more air traffic capacity to meet
projected needs. There was, however, almost no prior
consultation with the farmers, local officials, or representatives. The central government enjoys the power
of eminent domain, but the abrupt announcement of
such a major project did not sit well with locals, who
dug their heels in. Why locate an airport for Tokyo one-
hour's train ride from downtown? That is a question
many have asked ever since, but the rationale was to
reduce noise pollution in the capital, refocus Haneda
airport in central Tokyo toward domestic flights, and
to make Japan a regional hub for airlines by construct-
ing three runways. The Imperial Household Agency
made available a suitably large area of land in Chiba
Prefecture for the airport. This was most of the land
needed, but additional land adjacent to this massive
parcel was crucial to the project.

The insensitive and high-handed manner in which
the central government proceeded ignited a backlash.
Many of the farmers were veterans from WWII and
used those skills to thwart and delay the government's
plans and to offset the advantages enjoyed by state
security forces. They constructed barriers, tunnels,

bunkers, bamboo traps, towers, and huts to defend their land and slow construction. There was a degree of obstinacy among ordinary people who did not want to be pushed around by smug bureaucrats who just assumed that everyone would bow to their power and get with the program. Not these farmers, who got necessary support from many leftist student members of Chukaku-ha, who suspended their studies and relocated to these rural villages where their manpower was crucial, both for farming and demonstrating.

The New Left was reeling from the Asama-Sanso affair, but here was an opportunity for redemption. This was a rice-roots battle to defend land rights, but also drew on the sacral qualities of rice as a cornerstone of national identity, one threatened by modernization as manifested in the airport project. This growing disenchantment with modernization, fading traditions, and ruefulness over a "lost Japan" helps explains why the struggle to defy the state against the odds in the rice paddies of Chiba resonated so powerfully. Rather than overthrowing the capitalist order, scoring ideological points, or purging the ranks, the New Left found a mission in the politics of the daily, making a practical contribution to vulnerable communities bullied by the Establishment. It was also an environmentalist movement, drawing on popular concerns about the costs of runaway growth, an issue that put the Establishment on the defensive; in 1970 the LDP-controlled Diet adjusted to the public mood in passing strict new environmental regulations.

The delaying tactics pushed back the opening of the first runway until the end of the 1970s. The resource-fulness and resilience of the dissenters, and the plight of the farmers driven off their land, drew respect if not public admiration. But the airport was finally opened, a Pyrrhic victory for the state since the financial and reputational costs had risen dramatically. I recall my first visit in 1981 and being surprised at the scale of the security presence, the formidable maze of barriers, and the Darth Vader-like riot policemen. The battles intensified in the late 1980s with ongo-ing cat-and-mouse maneuvering between dissidents and security over airport expansion plans, transform-ing this civil aviation facility into what looked like an armed encampment with 6,000 riot police on hand. Currently, two of three planned runways are opera-tional, one shorter than planned because the author-ities were unable to secure use of key parcels of land. The remnants of resistance are still visible if you know where to look, but what was once contested ground has become just an airport.

Narita had all the makings of a white elephant pro-ject, testimony to poor planning and official inepti-tude. It is inconvenient for anyone going to Tokyo and for that reason lost passengers and flights to Haneda airport that has the enormous advantage of being right on Tokyo Bay, only 15 minutes to downtown. Haneda resumed international services in 2010, after a 32-year hiatus, expanding its facilities and runways on reclaimed land and making over its once dowdy facilities to re-launch as a 24-hour international hub. Narita never had a chance of becoming a regional hub because its landing fees are relatively high and restrictions on night flights makes it inconvenient. Thanks, however, to the post-2014 surge in tourism – suddenly Japan is one of the hottest global destinations – Narita is now bursting at the seams. It has added a third terminal for budget carriers and cut landing fees in a belated nod to market forces.

While it may not realize the grandiose ambitions of its planners, Narita is playing a vital role in the Japan boom as inbound tourism has more than quintupled since 2000 to over 25 million visitors in 2017.

## Anti-Nuclear Movement

The March 2011 meltdowns of three nuclear reactors in Fukushima prefecture are Japan's Chernobyl. Popular reaction to the Fukushima disaster was more immediate and massive in Europe where large rallies were held in Germany, and Italy held a referendum on continued use of nuclear energy. Governments in these nations responded to this public outpouring of anti-nuclear sentiments by declaring plans to eliminate reliance on nuclear energy. In Japan there were small anti-nuclear demonstrations in the spring of 2011, one gathering of 15,000 demonstrators on April 10, and a hardcore group bivouacked in Hibiya Park in front of the ministry responsible for promoting and regulating the nuclear industry, displaying anti-nuclear banners, but it seemed that the public reaction was relatively muted given the proximity of the stricken reactors to greater Tokyo's 30 million residents. One reason is that until May 2011, Tokyo Electric Power Company (TEPCO) and the government downplayed the severity of the accident and denied that meltdowns had taken place, and the domestic media was largely complicit in this cover-up. People were also overwhelmed by the scale of the disaster and were deeply concerned about the situation in the communities devastated by the tsunami, where tens of thousands of volunteers went to help in recovery activities. Over the summer, rallies grew larger as revelations mounted about institutionalized negligence, and the public became more aware of the plight of the 150,000 nuclear refugees that had fled areas surrounding the Fukushima plant.

Prime Minister Kan played a key and positive role in coping with the immediate crisis and defying the powerful nuclear village of government institutions, politicians, and the private sector that advocate and benefit from promoting nuclear energy. In May 2011 he pressured a utility to shut down the Hamaoka nuclear plant not far from Tokyo in what is considered one of Japan's especially high-risk seismic zones. The public overwhelmingly supported his July 2011 initiative to idle the nation's entire fleet of 48 operable reactors so they could undergo extensive safety tests. In exchange for his resignation, Kan also forced the Diet to adopt a feed-in tariff to promote renewable energy.

In September 2011, at Yoyogi Park in central Tokyo, about 60,000 people gathered to pressure the government to end reliance on nuclear energy. It was a festive and raucous atmosphere with placards, banners, and chanting demonstrators voicing their dissent. As this was the largest anti-nuclear rally to date, I expected extensive media coverage and thus was puzzled to see that on the evening NHK news, one of the most watched programs in the nation, there was no coverage at all. This is all the more surprising given that NHK's headquarters is literally across the street from Yoyogi Park. This is how dissent gets "unhappened."[11]

The slow burn anti-nuclear reaction erupted in the summer of 2012 as it became apparent the government just wanted to go back to business as usual and restart idled reactors. As of May 2012, all of Japan's reactors were offline, but fears that this might lead to a blackout proved unwarranted. When the DPJ-led government of Prime Minister Noda Yoshihiko (2011–12) gave the green light for the restart of two nuclear reactors in June 2012, he sparked a public backlash. People had become fearful of operating nuclear reactors in such an earthquake- and tsunami-prone nation and were concerned that the lessons of Fukushima were being ignored. The relatively small Friday evening protest rallies outside the prime minister's residence suddenly mushroomed from hundreds to tens of thousands every week from the end of June until September, mobilized on social media by the Metropolitan Coalition Against Nukes, a loose coalition of activist groups. In approving the reactor restarts, Noda back-pedaled from the anti-nuclear stance that his predecessor Kan had embraced with overwhelming public approval. Later that summer, Noda also waffled on his previous promise of a nuclear-free Japan by the 2030s, losing the DPJ's anti-nuclear support.

In December 2012, the LDP won the lower house elections and Abe Shinzo became prime minister for the second time. He was avowedly pro-nuclear, but led the party to victory mostly because the campaign was focused on economic and security issues, and because the public believed that DPJ-led governments were incompetent. The anti-nuclear movement persisted in 2013 with a few mass rallies, but attention shifted to opposing Abe's state secrets legislation that many feared would limit transparency and curtail press freedoms. The nuclear village weathered the perfect storm, but still faces judicial obstacles and a wary public.

## Managing Dissent

The "unhappening" of protest by ignoring it is a way that the media contributes to marginalizing dissent. For example, the protest movement against the dispatch of Japanese military forces to Iraq in 2004 in support of the American war effort drew almost no mainstream media coverage. This show of military support was very unpopular among Japanese because it seemed in violation of Japan's Constitution and did not meet the criteria set out in the Peacekeeping Operations (PKO) law that banned sending troops into a conflict area. But Prime Minister Koizumi (2001–6) was keen to show solidarity with the US to bolster the alliance and sent an engineering brigade to a relatively secure area in southern Iraq where they were guarded by Dutch and Australian troops. Demonstrations in Japan were not large, but fairly frequent. Speculation on why the media collectively ignored this story focuses on state pressure and worries that coverage might encourage others to join the rallies.

Less subtly, the government took disproportionate countermeasures to stifle dissent, conducting intensive surveillance on a small band of anti-war protestors in the Tokyo suburb of Tachikawa to intimidate them. In 2004, the "Tachikawa Three" were detained for 75 days and subject to extensive interrogations for trespassing and distributing anti-war flyers at an SDF housing complex. Amnesty International declared them "prisoners of conscience." The lower court dismissed the prosecution's case, but in 2008 the Supreme Court finalized the appeals court ruling that convicted and fined them for illegal intrusion.

Stereotypes notwithstanding, it is evident that not all Japanese are born conformists dedicated to preserving harmony, and for them there are less subtle enforcement mechanisms. Police rely on prolonged detention and interrogation of suspects to extract confessions. In the case of protestors, however, since they are usually detained on trivial charges, the detentions are more about quelling dissent through intimidation rather than winning a conviction in court. As mentioned in chapter 3, anti-base protestors in Okinawa have tried to block the planned relocation of a US Marine airbase from Futenma to Henoko, where construction of a new facility will cause extensive environmental harm.[12] They have also rallied against a new helipad facility in the tranquil forests of Takae, not only for environmental reasons, but also because Okinawa already bears a disproportionate base-hosting burden and they want to end the American military presence. One protest leader, Yamashiro Hiroji, 64 years old at the time, was detained for nearly six months between October 2016 until March 2017, denied visitors other than his attorney, and subject to interrogation without the presence of legal counsel. His "crimes" were to place cement blocks in the path of construction vehicles, cutting some barbed wire on a fence around a construction site, and shoving a Defense Ministry official. Under Japan's harsh criminal procedures, prosecutors can detain suspects for 23-day periods in endless succession provided judges agree, as they usually do. Yamashiro was a prominent protest leader who egged on demonstrators with his trademark megaphone and, by fearlessly standing up to authorities, inspired many others to do so. Detaining him on minor charges constituted arbitrary arrest, violating the International Covenant on Civil and Political Rights that Japan ratified in 1979. It is a practice usually associated with repressive authoritarian governments, not thriving democracies based on the rule of law. Apparently, the government is willing to risk looking like the former in order to silence influential protest leaders and warn other protestors what they risk by persisting.

## SEALDs (Students Emergency Action for Liberal Democracy)

In September 2015, Prime Minister Abe rammed controversial security legislation through the Diet that most Japanese opposed. These bills allow Japan to exercise the right of collective self-defense (CSD), meaning that under certain circumstances the SDF could be deployed to protect or assist the US in military action. Strong opposition to the new legislation is based on concern that sometime, somewhere Japan will be dragged into a conflict at Washington's behest that has nothing to do with defending Japan or its interests.

The massive demonstration in front of the Diet on August 30, 2015, involving well over 100,000 Japanese spanning the often-divided liberal spectrum and representing all generations, was a sign of the times. Demonstrators loudly denounced Abe as a threat to peace and the constitution, and there were many signs depicting him as a warmongering fascist and puppet of Uncle Sam. Although that evening's NHK 7 p.m. news declared it Tokyo's largest demonstration since the 1960s, the program devoted far more time to an investigation into faulty plastic stools and the dangers they pose.

Students were at the vanguard of this movement, attracting throngs of Japanese who shared their sense of outrage about Abe's trampling on Japan's constitution and pacifist norms. Peaceful youth activism is an encouraging sign in Japan's otherwise moribund political scene. The quixotic Students Emergency Action for Liberal Democracy (SEALDs) served as an inspiration for the nation, organizing demonstrations and arousing and instigating political engagement extending well beyond university undergrads. SEALDs are part of a post-3.11 continuum of protests by ordinary citizens angered by the Fukushima nuclear reactor meltdowns, Abe's 2013 secrecy legislation that undermined transparency and democratic values, government inaction in the face of racist assaults on the rights of resident ethnic Koreans, and rightwing vigilantism targeting the liberal media that in 2014 Abe publicly applauded in the Diet.

SEALDs was launched on May 3, 2015, Constitution Day, highlighting the group's concerns that Abe's unilateral July 2014 reinterpretation of Article 9, allowing Japan to exercise the right of collective self-defense, was tantamount to a stealth revision that ignored proper constitutional procedures. In doing so, Abe overturned the LDP's longstanding position on the matter. Okuda Aki, then a 23-year-old student at Meiji Gakuin and founder of SEALDs, insisted, "If one government can change things just with their interpretation, then the Constitution itself is altered and the government can do whatever it wants." Okuda, like many other SEALDs members, was often seen sporting a T-shirt emblazoned with "Destroy Fascism."

So what does SEALDs tell us about contemporary Japan? SEALDs was successful in terms of mainstreaming non-violent political activism and making it seem both cool and principled while giving a voice to the majority of Japanese incensed by Abe's high-handed tactics. Certainly, the students challenged the prevailing negative stereotype that youth today are politically apathetic, disengaged and retreating into the virtual world. The large and loud crowds that regularly gathered outside the Diet on Friday evenings in 2015 resulted from student activists rallying and mobilizing others to protect Japan's liberal democratic values. SEALDs managed to woo a public that shuns radicalism and extremist actions by renouncing leftist jargon, Molotov cocktails, police confrontation, and hunger strikes. Their moderate tactics were based on perceptions that the more confrontational style of protests and political agitation in the 1960s played into the government's hands, enabling it to portray them as extremists and thus deny the movement broader public support.

SEALDs sought to normalize political engagement and activism, drawing on the recent experiences of Taiwan (Sunflower Movement), Hong Kong (Umbrella Movement) and the US (Occupy Wall Street), and interacting with them. SEALDs' moderate manifesto, urging respect for the Constitution, liberal democratic values, and pacifism was part of a deliberate effort to distance the movement from the radical leftist protests of the 1960s. This drew criticism from some older leftists, but unlike more extreme groups, SEALDs managed to mobilize people from a wider demographic and their message resonated with a public eager to denounce the pronounced rightward shift in Japan's conservative political establishment.

It is striking just how media savvy SEALDs was with an English acronym, provocative placards in English, an English language website, press conferences, and attractive youth swaying to the drums while belting out tuneful chants. One of their attention-grabbing placards read: "I can't believe I'm still protesting this shit." They consciously wooed the international press, knowing that fame abroad translates into legitimacy and coverage at home. Their press outreach almost seemed professional, but strong self-presentation and multimedia skills come naturally to twenty-first-century youth. On its website, SEALDs displayed a cool coat of arms, with a quadrant depicting a book, a quill, a megaphone, and headphones with a play button icon in the center, demonstrating a canny sense of branding.

Despite winning respect, support, and kudos, SEALDs disbanded after fruitless efforts to unify the divided political opposition and mobilize voter support in the 2016 Upper House elections. They found it hard to influence mainstream politics and, in the end, Abe's conservative coalition won a commanding victory. In the following final chapter, we examine Abe's record and possible implications for Japan and its third transformation.

# Abe's Japan

Prime Minister Abe Shinzo is Japan's most polarizing leader since his grandfather Kishi Nobusuke was ousted from office in 1960, and is also not much liked by most Japanese, but has led the Liberal Democratic Party (LDP) to a series of electoral victories and is on course to become Japan's longest serving premier. In many ways he has been a transformative leader, but the results have been mixed.

Abe made a remarkable and unlikely political comeback following his humiliating ouster in 2007 after a shambolic year in office when he was nicknamed "KY" (*kuki yomenai* – clueless). Growing tensions with China over disputed islets in the East China Sea suddenly changed the battle lines of the 2012 election from a referendum on nuclear energy to one about national security. This favored Abe and the LDP because Japan's fleet of nuclear reactors was built on the LDP's watch and bilateral security ties with the US had grown frayed since the DPJ took power in 2009. The conservative LDP has dominated the Japanese political scene since 1955 and is known for promoting close security relations with the US, thus the escalating territorial rift with China propelled voters back to tested leadership. In many respects the DPJ looked

out of its depth, making little progress on its legislative agenda, while the public viewed the LDP as safe
hands at a time of crisis. Although the media declared
the 2012 elections a landslide victory, in reality the
LDP won more than one million votes less than in
2009 when it suffered a landslide defeat, suggesting
that Abe gained a relatively weak mandate.[1]

## Abenigma

"Abenigma" refers to Abe's puzzling political success.
How does a leader whose policies and leadership skills
are not held in high esteem maintain high levels of
public support and win four national elections in five
years since 2012? Typically, Abe's LDP wins about half
of the votes cast in elections where only half of eligible
voters turn out, meaning it is supported by only 25
percent of the electorate, but commands a two-thirds
majority in both houses of the Diet due to disparities in the electoral system. Abe's signature policies,
ranging from collective self-defense, arms exports,
and state secrets legislation to nuclear reactor restarts,
constitutional revision, conspiracy legislation, and the
Trans Pacific Partnership (TPP) are supported by only
about one-third of voters. National polls typically find
that support for his policies (15%) and leadership
(15%) is quite low while the main reason voters give
for supporting him is the lack of a viable alternative
(50%), hardly a ringing endorsement. That means his
support is fragile and depends on the weakness of his

opponents, not the merits of his agenda or personal virtues. Abe has been blessed by a weak field of rivals in the opposition and in his own party.

Still, it's hard to understand relatively high support rates, ranging from 40 to 50 percent, for a long serving premier whose eponymous economic policies of monetary easing, fiscal stimulus, and structural reform have not impressed the public. Indeed, an October 2017 Pew poll indicates that two-thirds of Japanese in their prime working age (30–49), say economic conditions are bad. Yet Abe campaigns successfully on the promise of Abenomics, offering a vision of hope, even though he has yet to deliver significant benefits for many households because wages remain stagnant and taxes have increased.

One explanation is that Abe's skilled PR team generates a constant flow of news and policy pledges, mostly controlling the media narrative while Abe strides assertively on the international stage, meeting more world leaders and projecting a more vigorous national image than any of his predecessors. Back in 2013 on a visit to Washington, DC, Abe boldly asserted "Japan is back," and he has worked hard to keep that promise. Abenomics entered the global lexicon and Abe was the picture of dynamic leadership, something missing since Prime Minister Koizumi departed the scene in 2006.

But Abe's popularity plummeted to 26 percent in the summer of 2017 as doubts gathered among Japanese about his credibility; 83 percent said they didn't believe his explanations about cronyism allegations that implicated him in two scandals. At that time, in a surprising departure from the usual reticence of former premiers, the LDP's Fukuda Yasuo accused Abe of incompetence and ruining Japan. Others lashed out at his strong-arm parliamentary tactics in passing controversial conspiracy legislation, charging he was arrogant and authoritarian. And Abe's protégé, Defense Minister Inada Tomomi, became embroiled in a cover-up involving the deployment of SDF "peacekeepers" in South Sudan during heavy fighting there in violation of the PKO law.

On the ropes, Abe called a snap election and managed a convincing victory because the opposition was in disarray and divided. This savvy gamesmanship, risking his two-thirds majority by betting that voters would prefer him, flaws and all, over new, untested opposition parties, demonstrated shrewd political skills. He also benefitted from the spectacular self-destruction of the opposition and some timely missile tests by North Korea that played to his national security strengths.

How has Abe used his power? It is remarkable that for a leader commanding a two-thirds majority in both houses for so long, Abe's legislative accomplishments in his first five years in office were modest, especially on urgent domestic issues. He has transformed Japan's security policy and endowed the prime minister's office with executive powers, but he has made less progress on economic reforms and very little on regional reconciliation, Japan's staggering demographic challenges, global warming, or gender bias in the workplace. His bold rhetoric injected some swagger into a nation reeling from the 2011 disasters and offered hope that the Lost Decades are over. In terms of identity politics, he rallied his conservative base by revising history textbooks, promoting patriotic displays, visiting the controversial Yasukuni Shrine, standing up to China, easing constitutional constraints on the nation's armed forces, and promoting constitutional revision.[2] While he has pursued an exceptionally active diplomacy, other than his sustained engagement with Russia, he has not charted new paths, mostly taking cues from Washington. He has only partially delivered on the vision of renaissance he conjured up during his early months in office. Even so, unlike many of his predecessors, Abe will not be a forgettable figure, if only because he understands the theater of politics and orchestrates it so effectively.

Abe's legacy agenda is constitutional revision, but this is complicated by a decidedly unenthusiastic public mood; in late 2017 just 6 percent cited this as a priority. The security threats posed by North Korea and China puts wind in his revisionist sails, but even though a vast majority of Diet members support revision in principle, there are deep divisions over the details of such revisions.

## *Abenomics*

Abe is said to have done a lot of soul searching following his 2007 exit, but more importantly he came up with a media campaign aimed to soften his hawkish, reactionary image. Instead of Mr. Constitutional Revision abandoning pacifism, he became Mr. Abenomics, promising economic revival in a nation that had endured prolonged economic stagnation. Abenomics was like a product launch, and immensely successful in generating a buzz about Japan. The three arrows (monetary easing, fiscal stimulus, and structural reform) drew on a Japanese proverb (about the advantages of unified action) that made a connection between traditional wisdom and contemporary needs, thereby wowing the global media. Anticipating the consequences of an Abe victory, and massive monetary easing, the yen nosedived and the Nikkei stock average soared even before he took office.

Much of what is touted as the success of Abenomics is due to the sharp devaluation of the yen. This boosted exports by making them cheaper in foreign currencies and increased the value of repatriated profits when converted into yen. The Bank of Japan's monetary easing and low interest rate policies involved purchasing over 40 percent of government bonds to the tune of $747 billion a year. It also helped orchestrate a share rally by acquiring 74 percent of exchange traded funds (ETFs) on the Nikkei stock index as of 2017 at a cost of $183 billion. In 2017 alone, it purchased $60 billion worth of ETFs and in early 2018 was spending $8 billion a month to prop up stock prices.

Abe's stated goal was to tackle Japan's longstanding deflationary mindset by targeting 2 percent inflation, but this objective has proven elusive. Deflation was declared the villain because consumers postpone purchases, anticipating prices will go down, and firms respond by lowering prices to entice consumers to buy, a dynamic that produces razor-thin profit margins. So, by deliberately stoking inflation through monetary intervention and fiscal stimulus, the government hoped to jolt consumers out of a deflationary psyche and nurture a virtuous growth cycle of soaring sales and profits, booming firms hiring more workers, raising pay and thus generating consumer confidence and onward and upward household consumption. This has not happened because the problem is thin wallets not a collective psychosis. Critics dismiss Abenomics as welfare for the wealthy, cutting corporate taxes, and pumping up the stock market while neglecting the needs of families, youth, women, non-regular workers, and retirees.

After five years of Abenomics, Japan's economy expanded by about $500 billion, more than the size of Belgium's GDP, and recorded the longest period of sustained growth since the mid-1990s. Not bad, but many competitors have done better in an era of global expansion. Export gains have spurred growth owing to robust demand from trading partners, while domestic consumption, the engine of growth in a healthy economy, has sputtered because wages and household income remain flat. With 27 percent of the population aged over 65 and 38 percent of the workforce relegated to low-wage non-regular jobs, deflationary pressures have been sustained by slack consumer demand. Even as many firms have posted record profits, they have been stingy with pay increases. In 2017 the World Economic Forum found that the fruits of growth have been unevenly distributed in Japan, ranking it 24th out of 29 advanced economies, Japan is also one of the worst countries in the developed world (25th) on intergenerational equality.

Abe's "three arrows" strategy suffers because the third arrow of structural reforms remains in the quiver. The first arrow of quantitative easing was welcomed as there are no vested interest groups that suffer while financial markets rejoiced that the Bank of Japan was underwriting guaranteed stock gains, reinforced by the government's decision to require the national pension fund to increase purchases of stocks. Fiscal stimulus, meaning increased government spending on public works projects and the like, helps construction companies and generates jobs in rural areas where longstanding LDP loyalists reside. Critics accuse the government of profligacy and assert that the massive public debt-to-GDP ratio of some 240 percent is mortgaging the nation's future, but the "let the good times roll" crowd of beneficiaries drowned out these doomsayers of austerity.

Analysts have called for extensive labor market

deregulation to make it easier to hire and fire workers,
but this has not happened. In 2018, following revelations about doctored data submitted to the Diet mis-
representing alleged benefits of "discretionary labor"
to workers that would have eliminated overtime
pay, Abe faced stiff resistance to his labor reforms.
In the end he managed to pass a package of reforms
that allows firms to eliminate overtime pay for certain categories of workers, and established a high cap
on overtime hours for others, raising concerns this
will boost *karoshi* rather than productivity. To counter labor shortages, Abe embraces "womenomics" as
the key to economic revival, and often talks about
empowering women, but hasn't delivered.[3] Women
remain concentrated in non-regular jobs (58%),
where wages are low, and it is stunning that there are
no women managers at 73 percent of Japanese firms
and that at listed firms only 3.7 percent of executives
are women.[4] He came into office boldly proclaiming
a target of 30 percent female managers by 2020, but
has since halved that target in the private sector and
pared it down to just 7 percent in the public sector.
He pushed through a gender equality law in 2015,
but since there are no penalties for non-compliance,
symbolism trumped substance. In politics, as of 2018,
only 47 of 465 Diet members are women, a lower pro-
portion than in Saudi Arabia, while there is just one
in his cabinet. In the gender equality rankings com-
piled by the World Economic Forum, Japan dropped
from 101st in 2012 when Abe came to power to

114th in 2017, the lowest ranking in the G7. He has made little progress on improving Japan's weak social infrastructure supporting families, meaning that for too many women, careers and raising children are an either/or choice.

Another major labor problem Abe has done little to address is Japan's relatively low productivity, in 2015 ranking only 20th out of the 38 member nations of the OECD, lagging behind Spain and Italy, and more than one-third less than the US. Manufacturing sector productivity is high, but 70 percent of jobs are in services, where Japan's productivity is low and decreasing, dropping by 10 percent between 2003 and 2016. This partly stems from greater reliance on non-regular workers, who are given little training.

The mediocre level of Japan's universities doesn't help. While Abe endorses making higher education free, he has done nothing to make it better. Japan is dead last in the OECD, investing just 3.2 percent of GDP in education compared to a group average of 4.4 percent. In terms of higher education, public financial support in Japan stands at a lowly 34 percent of total costs, less than half the OECD average of 70 percent. The benefits of higher education in a knowledge-based economy are well documented and essential to boost productivity, but in global rankings, and in Asia, Japan's universities are also-rans. In the 2018 Times Higher Education World University Rankings, for example, the University of Tokyo is ranked 46th and Kyoto University is 74th, while China has two universities in the top 30, and in the top 60, Hong Kong has three and Singapore two.

Another bellwether for the economy is the relatively low level of inward flows of foreign direct investment (FDI). In 2016 Japan attracted $11.4 billion, a paltry amount compared to the $254 billion invested in the UK and $395 billion in the US. In terms of attracting FDI, Japan is well below Spain ($30bn) and Italy ($29bn) and about the same as Poland and Turkey. This suggests that for all the hype, Abenomics has not done much to make Japan a more appealing destination for foreign investors.

## *Immigration*

Abe insists he will not tackle Japan's demographic problems via immigration. He has eased visa regulations to encourage small numbers of professionals in IT and finance to settle in Japan. This fast-track system for permanent residence is based on a merit point system, shortening the waiting period from ten years to five, but in the first five years since this system was launched in 2012, less than 10,000 applicants were approved, a drop in the ocean for a labor market of over 60 million. In 2018 Abe touted further immigration reform, but cautioned, "The prerequisite is that there will be a limit to the duration of stay and family members will basically not be allowed to accompany the workers."

The government has also expanded a back door

for temporary unskilled labor, mainly from Asian nations, under its technical training program. In 2017 about a quarter of a million such visas were issued, up 80 percent since 2011 and now the program includes health care services to alleviate shortages of elderly care workers. This program, however, has been plagued by a series of scandals, including excessive working hours, non-payment of wages, confiscation of travel documents, and debt bondage. The government estimates that some 80 percent of firms subject their trainees to labor law violations, but has not devoted sufficient resources to better monitor the situation and enforce relevant regulations. Vietnam has become the largest source of these trainee migrants, who ostensibly receive vocational training, but in most cases that is a polite fiction. Foreign students, some 240,000 as of 2016, have also eased labor shortages as many work up to 28 hours a week in convenience stores, restaurants, and other service industries.

More significantly, in 2018 Abe secured passage of immigration reform that opens the door to an estimated half a million unskilled workers by 2025 for up to ten years, but bars family members accompanying them and is designed to prevent them from attaining permanent residency. Severe labor shortages in certain sectors such as construction, agriculture, and health care propelled this reform. Even before this, the numbers of non-Japanese workers doubled to 1.3 million between 2012 and 2017 as the government has been pragmatic and flexible in adjusting to tight labor market conditions.

Advocates of immigration argue that it could solve lots of Japan's looming problems, especially a dire shortage of elderly caregivers, and that the 2.5 million non-Japanese currently in residence are not especially inclined to crime or disrupting local communities despite unfavorable media coverage. An influx could relieve labor shortages and migrant families could boost consumption, tax revenues, and support spiraling national pension and healthcare payments in a rapidly aging society where nearly a third of citizens are over 65 years old. But opponents point to the problems of unassimilated foreign enclaves in other nations that have become hotbeds of crime and unrest, and hype risks to Japan's social cohesion. Nobody in a position of power backs letting in the millions of migrants needed to make a difference; the UN projects that Japan needs to let in 381,000 immigrants a year, 17 million in total, until 2050 to maintain the same working age population as in 2005. The upshot is that immigration will not be a solution to Japan's evident problems because the scale necessary is unacceptable. Under Abe, Japan also continues to be indifferent to the plight of asylum seekers. Just 20 out of some 20,000 applicants were granted refugee status in 2017, and less than 1,000 in total have been accepted since Japan signed the UN Convention on Refugees in 1981.

## *Diplomacy*

Rather than the quiet diplomacy favored by most of
his predecessors, Abe has sought to play a catalytic
role and to advance what he thinks are national interests. He has cultivated closer ties with Southeast Asian
nations and Taiwan to counter a rising China, while
his overtures to President Xi Jinping have produced
little sustained momentum in improving bilateral ties.

Regaining some or all of what the Japanese call the
Northern Territories has been a major diplomatic priority for Abe. Japan doesn't recognize Russian sovereignty over these islands, helping to explain why the
two nations never signed a peace treaty. As detailed
in chapter 3, Abe has relentlessly courted Vladimir
Putin, meeting him more than any other leader in a
bid to cut a deal, despite the US policy of sanctions
and isolation. It is highly unusual for Japan to act in
defiance of US policies, but on this issue Abe was adamant. Alas, nothing came out of all his meetings and
it appears Putin never really intended to make any
territorial concessions and instead beefed up Russia's
military installations on the disputed islands during
the negotiations. A sticking point was whether or not
the US would be allowed a military presence on any
islands returned to Japan, something unacceptable
to Putin and awkward for Abe to negotiate given the
security alliance. Abe dangled investments and joint
resource development projects in the Russian Far
East, but these blandishments proved inadequate,

and it appears talks have reached a dead-end. Critics suspect that Putin's real aim was to drive a wedge between Tokyo and Washington.

As salesman-in-chief, Abe has promoted exports of Japanese nuclear power plants, infrastructure, and military equipment, all in a bid to promote growth, revive the economy, and to shed constraints that he thinks are outdated and holding back Japan, Inc. In this regard, India has been a much more successful gambit for Abe as he exchanged reciprocal visits with Narendra Modi, strengthened security ties, and helped land some major infrastructure projects, including high speed railways and industrial corridors. India is seen as a strategic counterweight to China and part of a containment strategy to restrain Beijing's hegemonic ambitions in the region. China and India have a long history of border disputes that erupted into war in 1962 and still percolate ominously, especially in the northeast region of India, most recently in 2017 over land claimed by Bhutan. Talk of "Chindia," extolling common interests in boosting ties, has receded; welcome news in Japan.

After prolonged negotiations, in 2017 Japan and India signed a civilian nuclear energy accord that allows Japanese firms to export critical components, undoing restrictions that had been imposed because India refused to sign the Nuclear Non-Proliferation Treaty and conducted nuclear tests. Despite concerns that Japan's technology could bolster India's nuclear weapons program, the deal gained Diet approval.

India's ambitious plan to build a fleet of nuclear reactors represents a potential lifeline for the beleaguered nuclear industry in which Mitsubishi, Hitachi, and Toshiba have been major players. Abe also concluded a $22 billion nuclear reactor deal with President Erdogan in Turkey, another earthquake-prone nation.

Abe pinned great hopes on his close relationship with Australian Prime Minister Tony Abbott, and at one point it seemed certain that Japan would snag a lucrative submarine contract that would have been Japan's first major arms export deal. However, Abbott was ousted and Japan did not win the contract, losing out to a French bid. The French bid won because their submarine better meets Australia's specific needs, and also because it addressed domestic political pressures to boost local production. This experience is part of a learning curve as Japanese firms begin to enter the global arms market. The self-imposed prohibition on arms exports was lifted in 2014 to facilitate Japanese participation in transnational joint development projects for weapons systems, but opens other potentially lucrative opportunities. While public opinion strongly opposed this change, Abe argued that it was overdue. He looks to increased military-related trade to help strengthen ties with other countries in the region that share Japan's wariness of China. This "arc of anxiety" stretches from New Delhi to Canberra, Jakarta, Manila, and Hanoi. Seoul is anxious too, but given unresolved historical grievances and a deep antipathy toward Abe among South Koreans, it is not considered a potential market for Japan's military exports.

## *US Alliance*

Abe emphasizes close security ties with the US, but had a strained relationship with President Barack Obama, mostly over issues of history, but they exchanged visits to Hiroshima and Pearl Harbor that demonstrated the possibilities for reconciliation that have eluded Abe with China and South Korea. In 2013, when Abe visited Yasukuni Shrine where war criminals are enshrined, Washington issued a sharp rebuke, because this gesture to his rightwing base imperiled US plans to strengthen trilateral security cooperation with South Korea, and was gratuitously provocative toward China.

Abe has cultivated closer ties with President Donald Trump, understanding that he rewards his friends and loyalty. Even before Trump took office, Abe rushed to Trump Tower for an audience, the first world leader to do so. He did Trump a great favor by telling the media he had a favorable impression at a time when the president elect's reputation around the world was dreadful. His handling of Trump was astute given his campaign comments quite critical of Japan on trade and security. Abe had already invested much political capital in bolstering the alliance and promoting the Trans Pacific Partnership (TPP), so he had a lot at stake in trying to woo Trump. Trump's erratic posturing left everyone guessing about his intentions and wondering whether his American First doctrine would cede power and influence to China in Asia and spark trade wars. But Japanese leaders cannot choose the president they have to deal with and Abe made the best of a difficult situation. On security, he got what he wanted: a US leader who would stand up to China and North Korea, endorsing Japan's vision of an open Indo-Pacific region to counter China's regional inroads.

However, Abe suffered three major setbacks in his personal diplomacy with Trump. Trump pulled the plug on the TPP in 2017 and despite pleading for an exception, Trump imposed tariffs on Japanese steel and aluminum exports in 2018. But it was Trump's abrupt volte face in 2018 regarding talks with North Korea that left Abe chagrined and isolated in his hardline stance opposing negotiations. It was a bitter pill to watch Seoul's envoys announce to the world from the portico of the White House that Trump had agreed to meet with Kim. He was upstaged by South Korean President Moon Jae-in's diplomacy and was marginalized by the summitry of North Korean President Kim Jong-un who first met with Moon, China's President Xi Jinping and President Donald Trump. Abe remained out of synch, insisting the talks prioritize the abduction issue, a reference to Japanese kidnapped by North Korean agents in the 1970s and 1980s who remain unaccounted for. Abe's political rise is closely associated with being an advocate for the abductees, and it is an important human rights issue, but averting Trump's "fire and fury" scenario for the Korean peninsula was a far greater priority for others. Abe's stance thus did not gain traction with Korean or Chinese counterparts, who wondered if he was more interested in scuttling the talks than making progress on denuclearization. Japan's main worry is that the talks will drag on inconclusively and effectively normalize North Korea's nuclear capability.

## *Abe Doctrine*

The Abe Doctrine has been transformative, but does not enjoy much public support, typically less than one third in public opinion polls. In acting as the Pentagon's man in Japan, delivering much more on longstanding demands than all of his predecessors combined, Abe shifted Japan toward a beefed-up military role, easing constitutional constraints along the way. Examples of his salami slicing strategy include siding with Washington against strong Okinawan opposition to plans for building a new airbase, lifting the ban on arms exports, and unilaterally reinterpreting Article 9 of the Constitution to allow Japan to engage in collective self-defense (CSD) that successive LDP governments had previously rejected and most constitutional scholars view as unconstitutional. Furthermore, in 2015 Abe signed new US–Japan defense guidelines that significantly expand what Japan is prepared to do in support of the US militarily, and passed legislation that summer that provided a legal basis for Japan's SDF to meet those commitments and engage in CSD. This concept means that not only can Japan's SDF defend the nation, but also allies and strategic partners who are under attack. The 2015 guidelines clarify that there is no geographical limit on where Japan's SDF are expected to engage in CSD, so this marks a significant departure from the previous 1997 guidelines that were restricted in scope to East Asia. Muscle flexing by China has helped Abe overhaul Japan's security policies and renounce the minimalist Yoshida Doctrine that had guided Japanese security policy since the 1950s.[5]

Commenting on Japan's evolving security posture, Kenneth Pyle, emeritus professor at the University of Washington, described Japan's post-1945 security policy as the "eight noes": no overseas deployments, no exercise of collective self-defense, no power projection capability, no nuclear arms, no arms exports, no sharing defense technology, no military spending above 1 percent of GDP, and no military use of space. Except for the nuclear option, Pyle said, now the noes are all gone. In 2017, Abe served notice of his intention to revise Article 9 in the Constitution, the "9th no." The nuclear taboo is also being questioned as North Korea's nuclear weapons program has sparked debate about the wisdom of Japan following suit, but only 9 percent of Japanese support such a move.

The Abe Doctrine, branded as proactive pacifism, is a potential game-changer because it lifts longstanding constitutional constraints on the Japanese military. Abe did agree to conditions that must be met before the prime minister can order military forces to engage in CSD, but the decision is left entirely up to the discretion of the prime minister without any obligation to consult the Diet. This enhancement of the prime minister's executive powers in security matters is unprecedented. Enhancing these powers, and boosting alliance cooperation and intelligence sharing, is also the purpose of establishing the National Security Council in 2013 and subsequent passage of the Special State Secrets legislation.

## *Executive Powers*

The Prime Minister's office has gained concentrated powers of appointment and promotion that grant the prime minister much more influence over the ministries and agencies, a politicization of the personnel system that has drawn sharp criticism for undermining the independence and credibility of the bureaucracy. In the US, the patronage system makes such executive office meddling a matter of course, but in parliamentary systems there is an inclination to insulate bureaucracies from politicization of appointments to maintain professionalism and institutional integrity. According to George-Mulgan, Abe built on a series of institutional innovations that have concentrated power in the prime minister's office and made it the locus of policymaking power, what she terms the "prime ministerial executive."[6] This is very different from the decentralized policymaking structure that prevailed since the US Occupation, fundamentally altering the distribution of power in the Japanese political system. Abe enjoys greatly enhanced authority and dominates like none of his predecessors, yet despite what George-Mulgan describes as "authoritarian proclivities,"[7] he has not had it all his own way, having to accommodate the demands of Komeito, the LDP's coalition partner, and pushback from public opinion.

In Japan, the Cabinet Legislative Bureau (CLB) offers legal advice about the constitutionality of proposed legislation so that it can be adjusted accordingly. It has enjoyed credibility because it has not been subject to political manipulation and had a reputation as an honest broker, respected by all sides. The Supreme Court rarely reviews the constitutionality of laws in part due to the CLB vetting of legislation; laws are not submitted to the Diet if the CLB disapproves. Knowing that the CLB has on numerous occasions rejected the exercise of the right of CSD, Abe intervened in the selection of the director in order to place someone in charge sympathetic to his views. This damaged the reputation and standing of the CLB, raising concerns that constitutional interpretations could be made at the whim of political leaders due to their policy preferences rather than legal precedents or principles. To the extent that the CLB renders decisions to suit the prime minister's wishes, respect for its opinions recedes. It is noteworthy that in 2015, former CLB directors testified in the Diet that Abe's CSD legislation is unconstitutional, meaning that the Abe Doctrine operates under a cloud of illegitimacy. So, in conceding that Abe has been a transformational leader with respect to security doctrine and establishing executive powers for the prime minister's office, there is considerable debate within Japan as to whether this is a positive legacy.

## Constitutional Revision

Abe's quest for constitutional revision is the reason he got into politics in 1993 and it is the legacy he seeks. He views the 1947 Constitution as a humiliating manifestation of Japan's subordination by the US, since Americans drafted it and made Japan dependent on the US for its security. This has been a bugbear for the rightwing in Japan, even if most Japanese embrace and value the norms and rights the constitution confers. Although rightwingers shrilly denounce the constitution, asserting it was imposed unilaterally and at odds with Japanese sentiments, public opinion has been favorable from the outset. Moreover, Japanese revised some aspects of the draft before it was debated in the Diet and adopted with overwhelming approval by Japanese legislators.

In 2007, Abe passed legislation that established the ground rules for a referendum on any constitutional revisions that are endorsed by two-thirds of both houses of the Diet. A simple majority in the referendum is required to enact any revision. During his second term, Abe initially downplayed his constitutional revision agenda and campaigned on Abenomics for the simple reason that most voters care about pocketbook issues and don't share his ideological zeal. But on May 3, 2017, marking the 70th anniversary of the constitution, Abe gave an interview with the conservative *Yomiuri Shimbun*, the newspaper with the largest circulation in Japan, in which he issued marching orders about what should be revised and how, setting a 2020 deadline for enacting such revisions. In doing so, he incited a strong backlash because he encroached on the prerogatives of the Diet that has the sole authority to decide on proposing revisions. Problematically, most Japanese oppose constitutional revision, and even for the minority that does support it, most oppose any revisions under Abe, highlighting his trust deficit. It is striking that over the past decade, polls indicate growing opposition to revision, a reality that forced Abe to limit his ambitions.

## *Press Freedom*

Freedom of the press in Japan has suffered under Abe. Carsten Germis, the German correspondent in Tokyo for the *Frankfurter Allgemeine Zeitung* between 2010 and 2015, was subject to harassment by Japanese officials who bristled at his critical coverage of Abe's revisionist history views. For Germans, the handling of wartime history is a sensitive subject and of great interest, so Germis wrote extensively about Japanese revisionism and efforts to promote a vindicating and exculpatory narrative. The Japanese consular general in Frankfurt visited the foreign affairs editor and complained about the critical coverage and asserted, without producing a shred of evidence, that Germis was getting paid by the Chinese to criticize Japan. Legitimate criticism of Abe and revisionism was disingenuously portrayed as Japan-bashing, implying that anyone opposing Abe's policies was somehow anti-Japanese.

The politicization of the news also gained momentum on the home front. In 2013, Abe appointed a crony with no media background to head NHK, the quasi-government broadcaster, and at his debut press conference he downplayed the comfort women issue and declared that if the government says right we can't say left, raising questions about his understanding of press freedom. Subsequently it emerged that the English language crew at NHK tasked with providing bilingual translation of news broadcasts was issued an "orange book" that detailed what words and expressions were taboo. For example, the expression "sex slaves" was prohibited and replaced by, "the so-called comfort women," Yasukuni Shrine should never be modified by "controversial," and other assorted euphemisms were imposed. On Abe's watch, four prominent television news anchors and commentators who were critical of him left their jobs in 2014–15.[8] These ousters sent a clear warning to other journalists about the possible consequences of critical reporting.

In 2017, David Kaye, a professor of law at the University of California-Irvine and the UN Human Rights Council's Special Rapporteur for Freedom of Expression, issued a damning report on press freedom in Japan. He expressed concerns about the vaguely worded Specially Designated Secrets Law, the potential for abuses, and how it might impinge on freedom of expression given inadequate protections under the Whistleblower Protection Act. Japanese journalists, media organizations, and civil society groups told Kaye about threats to the freedom of expression, including the "opaque and clique-plagued system of press clubs" that enforces norms of "access and exclusion," self-censorship, and access journalism. The latter encourages lapdog journalism to curry favor with those in power. For Kaye, it was striking that most of the many Japanese journalists who confided in him requested anonymity for fear of retaliation by their own management.

In Abe's Japan, organized rightwing campaigns of harassment and intimidation have become common. Reactionaries are confident that the prime minister has their backs, and indeed in 2014 Diet deliberations, he expressed support for an orchestrated campaign vilifying the liberal Asahi newspaper. This was extraordinary because some of those involved threatened violence against a former Asahi journalist and his family for his reporting in the 1990s about the comfort women. The university where he was employed was threatened with nail bombs if they refused to sack him. Significantly, Abe did not denounce these threats of violence or disassociate himself from the campaign.

Abe's press offensive came back to haunt him. Abe has long regarded the liberal *Asahi* newspaper, Japan's equivalent to the *New York Times*, as an enemy. Two pro-Abe newspapers, the *Sankei* and *Yomiuri*, launched simultaneous attacks in 2014 on the credibility of the *Asahi* over a handful of stories from the 1990s regarding the comfort women and on its critical reporting about the 2011 Fukushima nuclear accident crisis response. This orchestrated campaign caused a sharp drop in the *Asahi*'s circulation and it became notably less vocal in criticizing the Abe government. However, beginning in 2017, the *Asahi* led the media's pillorying of Abe over two cronyism scandals implicating him and played a key role in unveiling Defense Ministry cover-ups regarding controversial overseas troop deployments. The *Asahi* also exposed the doctoring of documents by the Ministry of Labor to support Abe's employment reforms and the redaction of documents by officials at the Ministry of Finance to obscure the role of Abe and his wife in a sweetheart land deal. As a result of these exposes, Abe's credibility and popularity suffered.

### *History*

New textbooks approved by the education ministry in 2015 show that there is reason to be concerned that accurate history is being sacrificed on the altar of Abe's patriotic education reforms. Nanking is no longer a "massacre" after being downgraded to an "incident," the Imperial military's role in instigating group suicides by Okinawans is obscured, and the comfort women are missing in action (MIA). The 1993 Kono Statement, in which the Japanese government acknowledged state responsibility for the coercive recruitment of comfort women, promised to teach the lessons of their sordid saga, but Abe has reneged on this pledge.

Abe advocates revising textbooks to reflect the revisionist history he favors. In this he has been enormously successful. During his first term (2006–7), he passed a patriotic education bill that required textbooks to conform to official narratives, giving momentum to a rightward shift in how Japan's wartime history is taught in secondary schools. By 2017, only one minor textbook included any reference at all to the comfort women, while none of the most widely adopted textbooks did so. That text includes testimony by a former comfort woman, but the publisher was required to include a disclaimer noting that her claims conflicted with the Japanese government's official view on the issue.

Back in the mid-1990s, every textbook covered the comfort women, but in the twenty-first century, there has been a wholesale retreat from a more forthright assessment of Japan's wartime misconduct. Progressives who lamented the whitewashing of Japan's wartime past decided to create a textbook option that provided information about the comfort women because none of the other textbooks do. Alas, private secondary schools that did adapt this text-book, some of the most prestigious and difficult to enter in the nation, were subject to an orchestrated campaign of harassment and deluged with threatening postcards.

## UNESCO Follies

Abe's assertive diplomacy has targeted the United Nations on several fronts, including rejection of complaints that he curtailed press freedom, criticisms over forced labor and the comfort women controversies, and the actions of the UN Economic and Social Commission (UNESCO). In 2016, the Japanese government announced that it would withhold paying dues owed to UNESCO, a $37 million expression of displeasure over the 2015 decision to include a Chinese submission on "Documents of Nanjing Massacre" in the Memory of the World Register. In doing so, the government was trying to pressure UNESCO into not accepting a comfort women dossier nominated by 15 organizations and institutions from 11 nations: South Korea, China, Taiwan, Japan, the Philippines, Indonesia, Timor Leste, the US, the UK, the Netherlands and Australia. This collective effort was a show of solidarity and also an effort to correct the misunderstanding that the comfort women issue is solely a bilateral problem with South Korea.

Japan's diplomatic hardball over such history controversies is counterproductive. In terms of global public opinion, opposing registration of the Nanjing massacre and comfort women dossiers makes it look like Japan is still in denial about the wartime past. In the end, Tokyo did pay its UNESCO dues, but unintentionally showed the world a glowering side of a reactionary leadership that is trying to minimize, marginalize, mitigate or shift responsibility for what was perpetrated. Sexual slavery is not unique to Japan, but what is the point of downplaying or denying a well-documented state-orchestrated, widespread system of deceiving and coercing tens of thousands of young women into providing sex to soldiers? The fact that other nations have not faced a reckoning for their war crimes is invoked to rationalize Japan's efforts at cover-up, but Germany provides a more inspiring model, as coming clean regarding wartime horrors has restored dignity to the nation and its victims while allowing it to regain moral authority.

In 2015, UNESCO accepted a Japanese submission on Soviet mistreatment of Japanese POWs, and conferred World Heritage status on a number of Meiji industrial sites, demonstrating that it is not inherently biased against Japan. Seoul withdrew its objections to the latter after Japan's ambassador to UNESCO agreed to the inclusion of signage at the sites about Koreans "forced to work" at these sites, but Foreign Minister

Kishida Fumio quickly dispelled any goodwill by insisting that "forced to work" does not mean "forced labor."

In 2017, the US withdrew from UNESCO, alleging an anti-Israeli bias, leaving Japan as the largest donor to the financially ailing organization. Japan used this leverage to gain veto power over any disputed dossiers submitted to the Memory of the World Register. Thus, UNESCO's integrity is now held hostage to the revisionist agenda of historical amnesia that Abe advocates.

Abe and like-minded revisionists of history are a bit like Donald Trump, living in an alternate reality where they can make up their own facts and dismiss inconvenient evidence. These revisionists dominate the ruling LDP, and rue Japan's reconciliation initiatives while advocating the rehabilitation of Japan's sordid wartime history in the mistaken belief that this will restore the nation's dignity. They want to roll back the apology diplomacy of Emperor Akihito, and a succession of LDP prime ministers in the 1990s. They undermine the 1993 Kono Statement and believe that the efforts of the Asia Women's Fund (1995–2007) to help former comfort women, and offer apologies, was a tragic mistake. They insist that the media's reporting about the comfort women has tarnished Japan's reputation rather than their own denials and evasions. In short, the national pride they seek to restore requires trampling on the dignity of the nations and peoples victimized by Japanese aggression and pretending like that never happened. Or, if that doesn't work, assert that everyone else did the same thing. This trumped-up version of Japan's history makes Japan look like its shirking the burdens of the past while its posturing on Pan-Asianism appears to glorify an ignoble quest to dominate Asia.

## Abe Statement 2015

Prime Minister Abe made a hash of his statement commemorating the 70th anniversary of the end of WWII. He was vague where he needed to be forthright – on colonialism, aggression, and the "comfort women" system – and came up short in expressing contrition by invoking apologies made by his predecessors without offering his own. Furthermore, Abe expressed perpetrator's fatigue, calling for an end to apology diplomacy. As a result, the Abe statement represented significant backsliding from those issued by former prime ministers Murayama and Koizumi in 1995 and 2005, which helped Japan and its victims regain some dignity while promoting reconciliation.

Emperor Akihito spent much of 2015 repudiating "Abenesia," making pointed comments about the need to address wartime history with persistence and humility. Constitutional constraints require him to avoid intervening politically, but he has been adept at navigating the gray areas in ways that have enabled him to become an influential advocate for reconciliation. There was a striking contrast in the respective

70th anniversary statements by Abe and Emperor Akihito, which highlighted the ongoing political divide between the revisionists and the understanding of most Japanese about how the nation got to where it is today.

Noting the deaths of innocent Asians across the region, including 3 million Japanese, Abe dog-whistled: "The peace we enjoy today exists only upon such precious sacrifices. And therein lies the origin of postwar Japan." This assertion that wartime sacrifices begot contemporary peace is a revisionist conceit, one that is conveyed in books and museums dedicated to sustaining the myth that Japan fought a noble war of Pan-Asian liberation and that the horrors endured were worthwhile.

Emperor Akihito offered a veiled rebuke on August 15, 2015, when he said, "Our country today enjoys peace and prosperity, thanks to the ceaseless efforts made by the people of Japan toward recovery from the devastation of the war and toward development, always backed by their earnest desire for the contin-uation of peace." Peace and prosperity, in the emper-or's view, did not come from treating the Japanese people and other Asians like cannon fodder during the war, but rather was based on their postwar efforts to overcome the needless tragedy inflicted by the nation's militarist leaders. He forcefully advocated a pacifist identity as the foundation for today's Japan, one that still resonates widely in Japan, challenging Abe's agenda of transforming Japan into a "normal nation," free from constitutional constraints on the military.

### Abdication and Succession

On August 8, 2016, Emperor Akihito, then 83, made a televised speech in which he conveyed his desire to abdicate, citing health problems, flagging strength and a desire not to inconvenience the nation. The announcement was something of a bombshell since the only other time he directly addressed the nation on television was to reassure the public and offer encouragement following the 3.11 tsunami and nuclear reactor meltdowns. Given his famously frosty relations with Prime Minister Abe and their divergent views on history and constitutional revision, there was speculation that the Emperor timed his announcement to slow moves toward the latter.

It was a remarkable speech that underscored what a punishing schedule this octogenarian maintained and his strong sense of duty to the Japanese people. There was an outpouring of sympathy and appreciation for all he has done over the three decades of his reign.[9] Akihito is greatly admired as the nation's chief emissary of reconciliation in Asia and as the consoler-in-chief at home, visiting those displaced by natural disasters and offering moral encouragement to the vulnerable and marginalized in society. He invented these roles and greatly expanded royal duties as he attended to the unfinished business of Emperor

Showa's (Hirohito) reign, when Japan's Asian rampage occurred, and connected with the people in ways that his aloof father never could. Making way for Crown Prince Naruhito allows a younger and more vigorous monarch to carry on in his footsteps. Oxford-educated Naruhito has a very hard act to follow, but all indications are, no doubt to the dismay of conservatives, that he shares his father's sense of mission and liberal outlook.

In Article 1 of the Constitution, the Emperor is designated as a symbol of the State and unity of the people, while Article 4 prohibits involvement in political matters. But Akihito came close to crossing that line by rejecting, subtly as he must, the option of a regency – the Crown Prince assuming his duties while he remained Emperor – and drew attention to the lack of any legal basis for him to abdicate under the current Imperial Household Law (IHL), implying the Diet should act. Trusted surrogates clarified His Majesty's desire that the Diet revise the IHL and establish a permanent legal basis for future abdications.

In the end, the LDP-led ruling coalition passed a one-off law in 2017 allowing Akihito to abdicate as an exceptional case, although an overwhelming majority of the Japanese public backed the Emperor's implied preference for a permanent arrangement. This would have required an amendment to the IHL, an option that had the backing of two-thirds of the public. So why not do what the emperor and public wanted? Patriarchy. The conservative Establishment that runs Japan worried that if the IHL was amended, this might lead to a public clamor to also allow for female succession. This, too, enjoys majority support among the Japanese, but is anathema to the old guard traditionalists. There have been empresses in the past, but not since the modern monarchy was established in 1868. Yet, there is a shortage of male heirs, so widening the pool to include females would seem a sensible risk management strategy. Akihito's son Naruhito succeeds him as Emperor of Japan in 2019, but he has no male heirs. His younger brother Akishino, however, does have a young son, Hisahito, who is the only next-generation male in line to succeed Naruhito. Much is riding on his shoulders since under the current system, once daughters marry, they lose their royal status. So, there was an opportunity for Abe to preserve and renovate the monarchy in line with public preferences and modern norms, but he failed to do so. Ironically, Abe grandstands on "womenomics" and the importance of empowering women in the workforce as a way to revitalize Japan, but given a chance to remove the glass ceiling in the imperial household, he balked. Nippon Kaigi (Japan Conference) is a powerful rightwing lobby group that seeks to rescind gender equality laws, revive the pre-1945 Imperial system and opposes female succession; most of Abe's cabinet ministers are affiliated with this group as are a majority of LDP Diet members. Apparently, they find no inspiration or comfort from the positive examples of

Great Britain's Queen Elizabeth or the Netherland's Queen Beatrix.

## *Wither Japan?*

Overall, Abe has been a transformative leader who has made significant headway on shifting national security policy away from pacifism despite public opposition. He has reinvented the institution of the prime minister, endowing it with significantly greater powers than any of his predecessors enjoyed. But the revamps he most yearned for, sweeping constitutional revision, remains elusive because the public is wary of his agenda and distrusts him. There has been a recrudescence of reactionary nationalism during the Abe era, but this has been a top-down phenomenon that has not resonated at the grassroots. Abe helped dispel the doom and gloom consensus about Japan's future that prevailed when he took office. Yet, few Japanese believe he has made Japan safer or ignited a sustainable economic recovery. He has done little to address gathering demographic challenges, relies on an ad hoc immigration policy that limits the potential benefits, and has not empowered women. He raised Japan's global profile, but made no headway in improving relations with China, South or North Korea, and came away empty-handed from his Russian diplomacy. Strengthening the US alliance will be remembered as his major diplomatic achievement, but in doing so he reinforced the client state relationship, ignored the democratic voice of the Okinawan people, gained the dubious distinction of being Donald Trump's closest friend among world leaders, and also heightened the possibility of putting Japan's troops in harm's way. There are also concerns among Japan's aid workers that their jobs in promoting human security all over the world have become riskier due to Abe's posturing and revision of the ODA (Official Development Assistance) charter that now allows aid disbursements for military assistance. The moral authority that Article 9 conferred has been weakened at a cost to Japan's soft power.

Perhaps the greatest global threat to human security is climate change, but on Abe's watch Japan has confined itself to modest targets for cutting carbon emissions by 2030 – only 18 percent from 1990 levels. In 2018 Foreign Minister Kono Taro acknowledged that Japan is lagging on renewable energy and said the government's energy policy is "lamentable" and out of touch with global trends toward de-carbonization. For example, Japan is exporting coal-fired power plants to developing nations, and is the leading financier of these projects, contributing to the spread of environmentally unsustainable development.

The 2020 Olympics present an opportunity for Japan to show off its extensive charms and remind people that it remains a vibrant nation boasting a zestful Gross National Cool. Abe, who appeared at the 2016 Rio de Janeiro Olympics as Super Mario, can take credit for boosting Japan's global image, a positive legacy of his artful showmanship that sugarcoats his reactionary agenda and deflects attention away from his flawed record and policy shortcomings.

In terms of Japan's third transformation, Abe has generated momentum on the economic and security fronts, but retreated on accountability, transparency, climate change, and regional reconciliation, highlighting the daunting tasks ahead as Japan continues to incrementally reinvent itself. Whether Abe can meet high hopes for a sustainable national rebound remains uncertain, and many are not enthusiastic about his agenda because it is seen to favor the privileged. His retreat from pacifist ideals is even more divisive. There is a consensus that Japan is past its peak and is in long-term decline, but this is a resilient nation with a track record of embracing change, overcoming misfortune and bouncing back, so it's hard to write off its prospects for coping with what now seem massive challenges. After all, who, surveying the ruins of Tokyo in 1945, would ever have imagined the phoenix rising from the ashes as spectacularly as it has?

# Further Reading

There is a rich literature on contemporary Japan that encompasses its nuances, dilemmas, foibles, and successes. Perhaps the best recent introductions are *Bending Adversity* (Penguin, 2014) by Financial Times editor David Pilling, who served as Tokyo bureau chief from 2002 to 2008 and, *Japan and the Shackles of the Past* (Oxford University Press, 2014) by long-term resident R. Taggart Murphy, a former investment banker and professor of business. Both authors' interests and expertise extend well beyond economic affairs with Murphy's analysis reaching from the feudal era to a critical analysis of the present-day US–Japan alliance, while Pilling focuses on contemporary society, including a poignant account of the March 11, 2011 tsunami.

The best book on the American Occupation (1945–52) is John Dower's *Embracing Defeat* (W.W. Norton, 1999), but I also highly recommend Eiji Takemae's *Inside GHQ: Allied Occupation of Japan and its Legacy* (Continuum, 2002). For those who prefer their history in graphic form, there is Mizuki Shigeru's magnificent four volumes *Showa: A History of Japan* (Drawn and Quarterly, 2014), covering 1926–89.

In terms of the Japanese economy, one is spoiled for

choice, but Chalmers Johnson's *MITI and the Japanese Miracle* (Stanford University Press, 1982) is a classic on the Japan, Inc. system, while Richard Katz examines what went wrong and why in *Japan: The System that Soured* (Routledge, 1998). Other excellent accounts abound: Richard Werner's *Princes of the Yen* (East Gate Books, 2001) is a superbly written analysis of the political economy of central banking, while William Grimes' *Unmaking the Japanese Miracle* (Cornell University Press, 2003) lucidly explains the botched macroeconomic policymaking that prolonged and deepened Japan's economic malaise. Richard Koo's *The Holy Grail of Macroeconomics: Lessons from Japan's Great Recession* (John Wiley & Sons, 2008) examines how firms collectively paid down their loans and stopped borrowing in what he calls the balance sheet recession. For the low down on environmental issues, see Timothy George's *Minamata* (Harvard University Press, 2001), while Jacob Schlesinger's *Shadow Shogun* (Stanford University Press, 1997) examines the dark side of Japanese politics. For an insider's account of Japan's dysfunctional democracy, see Gerald Curtis, *The Logic of Japanese Politics* (Columbia University Press, 1999).

In terms of security and the US alliance, the classic is Richard Samuels' *Securing Japan* (Cornell University Press, 2008), while Gavan McCormack takes a more critical stance in *Client State* (Verso, 2007). For more recent assessments, see Andrew Oros' *Japan's Security Renaissance* (Columbia University Press, 2017) and

Christopher Hughes, who provides a critical perspective in *The Abe Doctrine* (Palgrave Macmillan, 2015).

The edited volume by Yoichi Funabashi and Barak Kushner, *Examining Japan's Lost Decades* (Routledge, 2015), ranges widely over demographic, economic, security, and political issues, while a sense of the zeitgeist is powerfully delivered in Natsuo Kirino's superb novel *Grotesque* (Vintage, 2008). Richard Samuels' *3.11: Disaster and Change in Japan* (Cornell University Press, 2013) analyzes the limited policy impact of the disaster, while Richard Lloyd-Parry's haunting *Ghosts of the Tsunami: Death and Life in Japan's Disaster Zone* (MCD Books, 2017) is a masterpiece.

On dissent, and efforts to marginalize it, William Andrews *Dissenting Japan* (Hurst, 2016) covers the entire postwar era, while Noriko Manabe's *The Revolution will not be Televised* (Oxford University Press, 2015) focuses on anti-nuclear politics post-Fukushima. Anti-alliance politics in Okinawa are featured in Gavan McCormack and Satoko Oka Norimatsu's *Resistant Islands* (Rowman and Littlefield, 2012).

The Abe era and Japan's prospects are analyzed well in the multidisciplinary volume edited by Frank Baldwin and Anne Allison, *Japan: The Precarious Future* (New York University Press, 2015). On how Abe has consolidated political power, see Aurelia George-Mulgan, *The Abe Administration and the Rise of the Prime Ministerial Executive* (Palgrave Macmillan, 2018). Regarding Japan's biggest foreign policy challenge, see Sheila Smith's *Intimate Rivals: Domestic Politics and a Rising China* (Columbia University Press, 2015) and Giulio Pugliese and Aurelio Insisa, *Sino-Japanese Power Politics* (Palgrave Macmillan, 2017). *Japan's Foreign Relations with Asia* (Routledge, 2018), edited by James Brown and Jeff Kingston, provides a broader regional perspective.

# Notes

## Chapter 1: Bouncing Back?

1 Richard Lloyd-Parry, *Ghosts of the Tsunami* (New York: MCD Books, 2017); David McNeill and Lucy Birmingham, *Strong in the Rain: Surviving Japan's Earthquake, Tsunami and Fukushima Nuclear Disaster* (Basingstoke: Palgrave Macmillan, 2015).
2 Andrew Gordon, *A Modern History of Japan*, 3rd edn (Oxford: Oxford University Press, 2013); John Dower, *Embracing Defeat* (New York: W.W. Norton, 1999).
3 Beate Sirota Gordon, *Only Woman in the Room* (Tokyo: Kodansha, 1997).
4 I use Japanese name order: family name + given name.
5 Jeff Kingston, *Japan's Quiet Transformation* (New York: Routledge, 2004).
6 Mark Mullins and Koichi Nakano (eds.), *Disasters and Social Crisis in Contemporary Japan* (Basingstoke: Palgrave Macmillan, 2016).
7 Jeff Kingston (ed.), *Natural Disaster and Nuclear Crisis in Japan* (New York: Routledge, 2012).

## Chapter 2: Japan, Inc.

1 Chalmers Johnson, *MITI and the Japanese Miracle* (Stanford, CA: Stanford University Press, 1982).
2 Michael Schaller, *The American Occupation of Japan: The Origins of the Cold War in Asia* (New York: Oxford University Press, 1987).
3 Gordon, *A Modern History of Japan*.
4 Eiji Takemae, *Inside GHQ: Allied Occupation of Japan and its Legacy* (New York: Continuum, 2002).

5 Meredith Woo-Cumings (ed.), *The Developmental State* (Ithaca, NY: Cornell University Press, 1999).

6 Bradley Richardson, *Japanese Democracy: Power, Coordination and Performance* (New Haven, CT: Yale University Press, 1998).

7 Sadia Pekkanen, *Picking Winners? From Technology Catch-up to the Space Race in Japan* (Stanford, CA: Stanford University Press, 2003).

8 World Bank, *The East Asian Miracle* (Washington, DC: World Bank, 1993).

9 Roger Bowen, *Japan's Dysfunctional Democracy* (London: Routledge, 2003), Matthew Carlson and Steven Reed, *Political Corruption and Scandals in Japan* (Ithaca, NY: Cornell University Press, 2018)

10 Richard Katz, *The System that Soured: The Rise and Fall of the Japanese Economic Miracle* (New York: Routledge, 1998).

11 Ezra Vogel, *Japan as Number One* (Cambridge, MA: Harvard University Press, 1979).

12 Karel van Wolferen, *The Enigma of Japan* (New York: Vintage, 1990); Bill Emmott, *The Sun Also Sets: The Limits to Japan's Economic Power* (New York: Touchstone, 1989).

13 Timothy George, *Minamata* (Cambridge, MA: Harvard University Press, 2001).

14 Jacob Schlesinger, *Shadow Shogun: The Rise and Fall of Japan's Postwar Political Machine* (Englewood Cliffs, NJ: Simon Schuster, 1997).

15 Hiromasa Ezoe, *Where is the Justice?* (Tokyo: Kodansha, 2010).

16 Gerald Curtis, *The Logic of Japanese Politics* (New York: Columbia University Press, 1999).

17 Ethan Scheiner, *Democracy without Competition in Japan: Opposition Failure in a One Party Dominant State* (Cambridge: Cambridge University Press, 2006).

## Chapter 3: American Alliance

1 Bruce Stokes, Japanese Divided on Democracy's Success at Home, but value the voice of the people (Pew Research Center, 2017). Available at http://assets.pewresearch.org/wp-content/

uploads/sites/2/2017/10/04141151/Pew-Research-Center_
Japan-Report_2017.10.17.pdf

2  Gavan McCormack, *Client State: Japan in the American Embrace*
   (New York: Verso, 2007).

3  Chalmers Johnson, *Okinawa: Cold War Island* (Oakland, CA:
   Japan Policy Research Institute, 1999).

4  Laura Hein and Mark Selden (eds.), *Islands of Discontent:
   Okinawan Responses to Japanese and American Power* (Lanham,
   MD: Rowman and Littlefield, 2003).

5  Dower, *Embracing Defeat*.

6  Richard Minear, *Victor's Justice: The Tokyo War Crimes Trial*
   (Princeton, NJ: Princeton University Press, 1971).

7  Yuma Totani, *The Tokyo War Crimes Trial* (Cambridge, MA:
   Harvard University Press, 2008).

8  Kimie Hara, *Cold War Frontiers in the Asia-Pacific: Divided
   Territories in the San Francisco System* (New York: Routledge,
   2012).

9  James Brown and Jeff Kingston (eds) *Japan's Foreign Relations
   with Asia* (Abingdon: Routledge, 2018).

10 Amy King, *China–Japan Relations after WWII: Empire, Industry
   and War* (Cambridge: Cambridge University Press, 2016).

11 James Brown, *Japan, Russia and their Territorial Dispute: The
   Northern Delusion* (London: Routledge, 2016).

12 Monika Chansoria, *China, Japan and Senkaku Islands* (London:
   Routledge, 2018).

13 Robert Eldridge, *The Origins of US Policy in the East China Sea
   Islands Dispute: Okinawa's Reversion and the Senkaku Islands*
   (New York: Routledge, 2014).

14 Thomas French, *National Police Reserve: The Origin of Japan's
   Self Defense Forces* (Leiden: Brill, 2014).

15 Richard Samuels, *Securing Japan: Tokyo's Grand Strategy and
   the Future of East Asia* (Ithaca, NY: Cornell University Press,
   2008).

16 Ichiro Ozawa, *Blueprint for a New Japan: The Rethinking of a
   Nation* (Tokyo: Kodansha, 1994).

17 Andrew Oros, *Japan's Security Renaissance: New Policies and
   Politics for the 21st Century* (New York: Columbia University
   Press, 2017).

18 Robert Boynton, *The Invitation-Only Zone: The True Story of North Korea's Abduction Project* (New York: Farrar, Straus and Giroux, 2016).

19 Peng Er Lam, *Japan's Relations with Southeast Asia: The Fukuda Doctrine and Beyond* (New York: Routledge, 2012).

20 R. Taggart Murphy, *Japan and the Shackles of the Past* (Oxford: Oxford University Press, 2015).

21 Christopher Hughes, *The Abe Doctrine* (Basingstoke: Palgrave Macmillan, 2015).

22 Oros, *Japan's Security Renaissance*.

## Chapter 4: Lost Decades and Disasters

1 Emmott, *The Sun Also Sets*.

2 Stephen Vogel, *Japan Remodeled: How Government and Industry Are Reforming Japanese Capitalism* (Ithaca, NY: Cornell University Press, 2006).

3 Leonard J. Schoppa, *Race for the Exits: The Unraveling of Japan's System of Social Protection* (Ithaca, NY: Cornell University Press, 2006).

4 Anne Allinson, *Precarious Japan* (Durham, NC: Duke University Press, 2013).

5 David Edgington, *Reconstructing Kobe: The Geography of Crisis and Opportunity* (Vancouver, BC: University of British Columbia Press, 2011).

6 Ian Reader, *Religious Violence in Contemporary Japan: The Case of Aum Shinrikyo* (Honolulu: University of Hawaii Press, 2000).

7 William Pesek, *Japanization: What the World Can Learn from Japan's Lost Decades* (Singapore: John Wiley & Sons, 2014).

8 Richard Koo, *The Holy Grail of Macroeconomics: Lessons from Japan's Great Recession* (Singapore: John Wiley & Sons, 2009).

9 Naoyuki Yoshino and Farhad Taghizadeh-Hesary, *Japan's Lost Decade: Lessons for Asian Economies* (New York: Springer, 2017).

10 Dennis P. J. Botman, Stephan Danninger, and Jerald Schiff, *Can Abenomics Succeed? Overcoming the Legacy of Japan's Lost*

Decades (Washington, DC: International Monetary Fund, 2015).

11 David Chiavacci and Carola Hommerich (eds.), *Social Inequality in Post-Growth Japan: Transformation during Economic and Demographic Stagnation* (London: Routledge, 2016).

12 Yoichi Funabashi and Barak Kushner, *Examining Japan's Lost Decades* (New York: Routledge, 2015).

13 Jeff Kingston (ed.), *Press Freedom in Japan* (New York: Routledge, 2017).

14 Jeff Kingston, *Contemporary Japan*, 2nd edn (Oxford: Wiley-Blackwell, 2013).

15 Kiyoto Tanno, *Migrant Workers in Contemporary Japan* (Melbourne: Trans Pacific Press, 2014).

16 David Chapman, *Zainichi Korean Identity and Ethnicity* (London: Routledge, 2007).

17 Toshiaki Tachibanaki, *Confronting Income Inequality in Japan* (Cambridge, MA: MIT Press, 2009).

18 Huiyan Fu, *An Emerging Non-Regular Labour Force in Japan* (New York: Routledge, 2015).

19 Frank Baldwin and Anne Allinson (eds.), *Japan's Precarious Future* (New York: New York University Press, 2015).

20 Ellis Krauss and Robert Pekkanen, *The Rise and Fall of Japan's LDP* (Ithaca, NY: Cornell University Press, 2010).

21 Robert Pekkanen, Steve Reed and Ethan Scheiner (eds.), *Japan Decides 2012* (Basingstoke: Palgrave Macmillan, 2013).

22 Kingston (ed.), *Natural Disaster and Nuclear Crisis in Japan*.

23 David Lochbaum, Edwin Lyman, Susan Q. Stranahan and the Union of Concerned Scientists, *Fukushima: The Story of a Nuclear Disaster* (New York: The New Press, 2015).

24 Richard Samuels, *3.11: Disaster and Change in Japan* (Ithaca, NY: Cornell University Press, 2013).

## Chapter 5: Dissent

1 Keiko Hirata and Mark Warschauer, *Japan: The Paradox of Harmony*. (New Haven, CT: Yale University Press, 2014).

2 Ivan Morris, *The Nobility of Failure: Tragic Heroes in the History of Japan* (Fukuoka: Kurodahan Press, 2013).

3 Dower, *Embracing Defeat*.

4 Takemae, *Inside GHQ*.

5 Frank Packard, *Protest in Tokyo: The Security Treaty Crisis of 1960* (Princeton, NJ: Princeton University Press, 1966).

6 William Andrews, *Dissenting Japan: A History of Japanese Radicalism and Counterculture from 1945 to Fukushima* (London: Hurst, 2016).

7 David Apter and Nagayo Sawa, *Against the State: Politics and Social Protest in Japan* (Cambridge, MA: Harvard University Press, 1984).

8 Manabu Miyazaki, *Toppamono: Outlaw, Radical, Suspect: My Life in Japan's Underworld* (Tokyo: Kotan, 2005).

9 Johnson, *Okinawa: Cold War Island*.

10 The Weather Underground (1969–77) was a militant leftist organization founded at the University of Michigan with the goal of overthrowing the US government.

11 Noriko Manabe, *The Revolution will not be Televised: Protest Music after Fukushima* (Oxford: Oxford University Press, 2015).

12 Gavan McCormack and Satoko Oka Norimatsu, *Resistant Islands: Okinawa Confronts Japan and the United States* (Lanham, MD: Rowman and Littlefield, 2012).

## Chapter 6: Abe's Japan

1 Pekkanen et al. (eds.), *Japan Decides 2012*.

2 Arthur Stockwin and Kweku Ampiah, *Rethinking Japan: The Politics of Contested Nationalism* (Lanham, MD: Lexington Books, 2017).

3 Kumiko Nemoto, *Too Few Women at the Top: The Persistence of Inequality in Japan* (Ithaca, NY: Cornell University Press, 2016).

4 BBC, "Reality Check: Has Shinzo Abe's 'womenomics' worked in Japan?" (February 17, 2018). Available at: http://www.bbc.com/news/world-asia-42993519

5 Sheila Smith, *Intimate Rivals: Domestic Politics and a Rising China* (New York: Columbia University Press, 2015).

6 Aurelia George-Mulgan, *The Abe Administration and the*

*Rise of the Prime Ministerial Executive* (Palgrave Macmillan, 2018)

7  Ibid.
8  Kingston (ed.), *Press Freedom in Japan.*
9  Kenneth Ruoff, *The People's Emperor: Democracy and the Japanese Monarchy 1945–1995* (Cambridge, MA: Harvard University Press, 2003).

# Index